INDIVIDUALIZED STUDY

INDIVIDUALIZED STUDY

A New Approach to Succeeding in College

GERALD A. GLADSTEIN

University of Rochester

RAND McNALLY & COMPANY • **CHICAGO, ILLINOIS**

RAND McNALLY EDUCATION SERIES

B. OTHANEL SMITH, *Advisory Editor*

To
Barbara

AUTHORS WRITE BECAUSE THEY BELIEVE THEY have something important to say. I am no exception. I have written this book because I believe that college students face great problems and that they need help in solving these problems.

There are many sources of data to support this statement. However, I shall rely only on two: the figures available on college failures and dropouts, and my personal experiences while working with college students during the past ten years. Concerning the former, it is sad, but true, that about half the students who start college in this country do not graduate. Although the figure on failures and dropouts varies from college to college, in most four-year colleges about 50 per cent of the students who enter college do not finish their programs in the prescribed time. This fact is disturbing. More upsetting, however, is the realization that this proportion of failures has remained constant during the past thirty years! Despite our increased scientific knowledge in many areas—rockets, antibiotic drugs, food preservation—we have been unable to reduce the failure rate of college students.

This does not mean that we have not advanced in our knowledge of how people learn. Quite the contrary—we know much more about the process of learning today than we did thirty years ago. Our problem is that we have not been able to help the college student apply this knowledge.

Thus, I now turn to my second source of data concerning the college student's problems. As a college teacher and counselor, I have worked with hundreds of students attempting to succeed. Some were extremely bright, eager freshmen who lost interest by the end of the second semester. Some were poorly prepared sophomores, faced with low levels of achievement and struggling to stay in college. Others were academically successful juniors who were confused about their goals in life. Still others were seniors who were anxious about their post-college plans. Regardless of their year in college, they were all faced with achieving their own particular types of success. Each was trying to solve problems that many other college students have encountered, and, at the same time, to resolve a problem unique to himself. No two students have quite the same difficulties.

These three observations—that the failure rate of college students is still tremendously high, that the college student does not profit from our new knowledge in the area of learning, and that each student is struggling to solve a problem unique to himself—became the basis for this book. Simply stated, I have tried to translate our recent findings concerning learning in such a manner that you, the student, can understand and apply them to yourself.

Central to my presentation is our knowledge of *individual differences*. In contrast to many books concerned with helping college students, I have not identified and discussed one basic method of approaching college work. Instead, I have assumed that individual differences among college students are so important that each student must evolve a method appropriate to himself and his college. Thus, the discussions and practice activities have been developed to help you create, test, and revise your own procedures for succeeding in college.

As you carry out this process, you will have to apply other crucial learning concepts. You will analyze your *motivation*. You will have to become aware of certain *personality factors* and their impact on your attempts to succeed. You will look at your *habits, attitudes, personality needs,* and *unconscious factors*. Equally significant, you will try to discover the relationship of these non-intellectual factors to your *abilities* and the *types of learning* which you use.

To help you apply these concepts, I have developed numerous practical activities. As you do these, you will have to apply another basic learning concept—*supervised practice*. If you complete the activity sheets as you go along, by the time you reach the end of the book you will find that you will have made a careful analysis of yourself and of your college, identified needed self-improvements, and developed an individual plan of action:

You will have applied our knowledge of learning to yourself.

To facilitate this process, I have written the book in an informal style. I have assumed that you will better understand these abstract learning concepts if I "talk" with you as if you were a student coming in to see a counselor, and accordingly, I hope you will carry on a "conversation" with me as you read and study the material.

The ideas that I have developed in this book have not evolved in a vacuum. Of the many people who have directly or indirectly affected my thinking, two of my former professors have been especially influential: Dr. Benjamin S. Bloom helped me grasp the tremendous importance of the interaction of the individual with his particular environment. This book is based upon this concept. Dr. Carl R. Rogers helped me understand a basic philosophical approach to helping people, and his belief in the individual's potential for helping himself is also incorporated in this book. I must also express my appreciation to my former students and counselees, whose reactions to my ideas and my efforts to help them have also greatly influenced me. In a sense, the content of this book has evolved from my experiences with them.

Also, I am very appreciative of the time, energy, and ideas contributed by students and colleagues who read the manuscript and offered helpful criticisms, particularly Kenneth Daniels, Myra Friedman, Valerie Harrison, Susan Johnson, Thomas Knapp, Seth Leibler, Jan Meades, Deanne Molinari, Harold Munson, Patricia Nicolaides, Carol Oliver, Robert Sally, Kathleen Shea, William Stryker, Ivan Tomanovich, and Barbara Turner.

Finally, I am especially grateful to my family who, despite the anguish involved in having a writer in the family, have encouraged and facilitated the book's ideas and completion.

TABLE OF CONTENTS

SECTION ONE

Learning about Yourself and Your College

CHAPTER I

You and Your College Are Unique

SINCE YOU HAVE BEGUN TO READ THIS BOOK, may we assume that you want to succeed in college? But what do you mean by success? Are you referring to getting good grades, making the varsity football team, getting into the proper sorority, or learning how to think critically?

Success, you see, can mean different things to different people. You may be primarily concerned with scholastic achievement, while your best friend may be more involved with social achievement. Regardless of the type or types of success you desire, one thing is sure—achieving success of any kind in college is a complicated process. Because

college is different from high school in many ways, this process of achieving success during college may well be different from the process you have followed earlier. You will probably encounter new unknowns and higher standards. Thus, the methods you have used to succeed in high school may no longer be sufficient for you to succeed in college.

Moreover, there is another complicating factor. You may be changing your ideas of what constitutes success. Perhaps social or athletic success is more important to you now than it was in your high school days; on the other hand, it may be that you are now giving more attention to economic, artistic, or occupational concerns.

SUCCESS DEPENDS UPON YOU

Regardless of the type of success you now desire (we shall have more to say about this later), I think we can agree on one basic point—this success will depend primarily on *you*! Let's talk about this a bit. During your younger years you probably leaned heavily upon your parents and teachers. Since then, however, you have probably wanted to be on your own more: to make your own decisions and plan your own future. This change is quite common and, for most adolescents, quite healthy. Yet you should realize that this greater freedom and responsibility means that you won't be able to depend as much now as in the past upon help from others in your efforts to succeed.

This thought may be either challenging or frightening to you, or perhaps both. It may also lead you to search for easy solutions to your problems regarding success. With your parents and former teachers unavailable for guidance, you may want to seek out quick solutions. And yet, I'm sure you will agree, it is foolish to expect to find easy ways to succeed in college. As we shall see later, colleges and students are different enough to make it difficult, if not impossible, to find simple formulas for success which will apply to all students. Rather, we should expect there to be many possible solutions, depending upon the particular student and the particular college he is attending.

So your success will depend primarily on you. You will have to choose from the many possible means of succeeding and make a deliberate effort to arrive at the solutions which are best for you. This means that you need to understand thoroughly what you mean by success, what kind of person you are, and the ways you have tried to succeed in the past. It also means that you must thoroughly understand your particular college situation, its requirements and its oppor-

tunities. In addition, you must know, and be able to use, various ways of succeeding so that you can apply them to yourself as you attend college.

You may be asking yourself at this point: But how can I learn more about myself, my college, and the various ways of succeeding? I hope I can be of help to you here. Throughout this book I shall try to help you arrive at the best solutions for *you*. I hope we can work together in helping you to know yourself better, to understand your college, and to apply many ideas that can help you. As a start, let's look at yourself and your college a bit more thoroughly.

YOUR UNIQUENESS IS IMPORTANT

As you look at yourself you will notice that you are like other students in many ways. You have the same *kinds* of abilities, interests, and achievements. For example, you share with others some degree of scholastic, social, and mechanical abilities, some interests, and some achievements. Likewise, you have some of the same *kinds* of personality characteristics, attitudes, and values. These include some degree of personality adjustment, certain personality needs, particular attitudes toward authority, and certain values regarding private property or honesty.

Since you share with other students these same kinds of characteristics and qualities, you can compare yourself with them. In other words, you have more in common with a group of college students, let us say, than with a group of elementary school children or adults. The fact that you share common qualities with other adolescent students is very important, because you will be able to use this knowledge later in trying to determine the best ways of succeeding for *you*.

At the same time, however, you cannot overlook the fact that you are also *different* from all other students. Your abilities, interests, achievements, personality characteristics, attitudes, and values are *not* exactly the same as any other student's. Because you possess a particular combination of characteristics, you are an individual. *You are unique!* This uniqueness is important—because it influences the type of success which *you* seek and the type of methods that *you* must use to achieve this success. Your knowledge of your uniqueness will also be valuable later, when you try to determine the best ways of succeeding for you.

YOUR COLLEGE'S UNIQUENESS IS IMPORTANT

Just as you share many common characteristics with other students, so your college shares many characteristics with other colleges. It has some of the same physical elements (classrooms, laboratories, libraries, residence halls, and so on), academic and non-academic requirements, and learning opportunities, and it probably has similar grading practices, class responsibilities, degree requirements, residence hall regulations, and special events. These common qualities allow you to compare your college to other colleges and help you to determine the best ways of succeeding at your college or any other.

However, your college is also different from all other colleges. Because its physical elements, academic and non-academic regulations, and learning opportunities are not exactly the same as any other college's, *it* is individualistic or unique too. Your knowledge of its uniqueness is just as important as your knowledge of your own uniqueness. You must understand its individuality if you are to find the best ways of obtaining success.

YOU MUST UNDERSTAND YOURSELF AND YOUR COLLEGE

Before we go any further, let's see if we agree on several basic points. Do you agree that

1. You have your own way of thinking about success.
2. The success you want may or may not be the same as what other college students want.
3. Your success in college will depend primarily on you (not on your parents, teachers, and so on).
4. You are similar to, but different from, all other college students.
5. Your uniqueness is important to your success in college.
6. Your college is in some respects similar to, but also different from, all other colleges.
7. Your college's uniqueness is important to your success in college.

If you agree with these statements, then we can proceed to the next step. Since both you and your college are unique, you must understand both. You must be able to compare what you mean by success and what your college means by success. If you and your college are both striving for the same type of success, then you must compare the particular requirements of your college and your unique qualities for meeting these requirements.

On the other hand, if you and your college are *not* striving for the same type of success, then you are faced with a different problem. Should you change what you are striving for, or go along with what the college wants? If you decide not to change, what happens then? If you decide to change, what methods must you use to achieve this new type of success?

In other words, you must understand what may happen when you attempt to achieve the type of success you want in your college. You must understand both yourself and your college.

THE FUNCTION OF THIS BOOK

The rest of this book is devoted to helping you achieve this understanding. I shall begin by trying to help you gain a better comprehension of your uniqueness and your college's individuality. Then we shall look at the specific courses you are taking, and I shall help you analyze the particular requirements of each. In contrast to many authors, however, I shall *not* tell you to use *one* method of study; rather, I shall try to help you understand the *various ways* you can study to meet these requirements. Finally, I shall help you to select and develop the study methods *best for you* and your courses.

CHAPTER II

Some Necessary Precautions

BEFORE PROCEEDING WITH YOUR ANALYSIS OF yourself and your college, it is important to step back and notice some problems that you may encounter. Looking at yourself analytically is not an easy thing to do; therefore, let's pause and look at some possible difficulties.

WATCH OUT FOR THE ROADBLOCKS

Difficulties may occur because of certain restricting conditions or roadblocks. *If you do not look at these roadblocks now, you may not be able to obtain any better understand-* *ing of yourself than you now have.* Putting it another way, if you can avoid the roadblocks, your chances of succeeding will be better.

What are these conditions or roadblocks that can interfere with your success? They include habits, attitudes, personality needs, and unconscious factors. Although we all possess these conditions or factors, most of us are *unaware* of how they influence our attempts to succeed. In themselves they are not roadblocks, but *certain* habits, attitudes, personality needs, and unconscious factors may interfere with your attempts to succeed. That is why it is so important, at this point, for you to understand the nature of these conditions and how they are *now* influencing you.

YOU ALREADY HAVE SOME WELL ESTABLISHED HABITS

The first potential roadblock arises in your habits. You probably have known for a long time that you have certain habits, but what are habits? Why do we develop and keep habits? Why is it hard for us to change habits?

A habit is an established way of doing something. You do this thing almost automatically. Thus, if you have a certain eating habit, you will eat in a set way without thinking about it. All of us have various kinds of habits. These include mental, social, and physical habits. *Mental habits* refer to those behaviors, which you carry out automatically, that are primarily based upon the mind and its intellectual processes. Ways of thinking and of studying are mental habits. *Social habits* refer to those behaviors, carried out automatically, that are primarily based upon the non-intellectual aspects of the personality and to the way in which you use them in social situations. Examples are expressing emotions and frustrations habitually in the presence of others. *Physical habits* refer to those behaviors, which you carry out automatically, that are primarily based upon the body and its movements. Examples are your eating and walking habits.

Regardless of its type, *a habit is acquired over a period of time.* It becomes established when a kind of behavior or set of behaviors is repeated over and over again. *Typically, this habit is established because you discover (knowingly or unknowingly) that carrying it out gives you more pleasure than pain.* For example, you may develop a certain dressing habit—a way of tying your shoes. You tie your shoes almost automatically (by habit), since this makes it easier for you to dress yourself. If you had not developed this habit,

you would have to think about how to tie your shoes each day. Since this would require considerable time and energy, it would be "painful"; it would take time from doing other things. Therefore, since it gives you more pleasure than pain to tie your shoes habitually, you have developed this particular dressing habit.

We can see the same development in intellectual habits. Let's take reading. If you always read in a certain way, you can say you have a reading habit. How have you acquired this habitual way of reading? The answer lies, probably, in your early years in elementary school. As you learned to read, you discovered that reading in a certain way gave you more pleasure than pain. We are not talking here about how much you enjoyed reading; rather, we are interested in the results that occurred as a result of the way you read.

If you learned to read well, you probably received praise from your teachers and parents. This gave you pleasure and, therefore, you continued to read in this way. After a while, this method developed into a habit. If you had difficulty in learning to read, you probably attempted to read in more than one way. After a while, you discovered that one of these ways was less painful (your teachers and parents punished you less or praised you more), and, therefore, you continued to read in this way until this kind of reading became established as a habit. Although you may not have obtained pleasure from this reading habit, you have avoided additional pain—therefore, you have kept the habit.

Thus, *typically you develop habits without realizing it.* The process occurs so naturally that you do not become aware of your habits until you analyze what you are doing. This is one of the reasons why it is so hard to change habits. Because you don't understand how you acquired a habit, it is hard for you to undo or reverse the learning. In addition to this, you may have difficulty in changing habits because they have given you more pleasure than pain. In other words, in order for you to change habits, you have to experience more pain, at least temporarily, than pleasure. Of course, once you get through that initial stage of additional pain, you will then derive more pleasure from the new habit which improves upon the old.

In illustration, let's look at a common habit—smoking. If you smoke habitually, you probably developed this habit in your early teen years. What pleasure did you receive? Probably you liked the taste of the cigarette. In addition, you probably felt "grown up" and accepted by your friends. You may also have developed the habit of smoking at certain times: after eating, while talking to friends, while reading or watching television, and so on. In all likelihood, you did not realize at the time what kind of smoking habit you were developing.

If you have tried to stop smoking or change your smoking habits, you may well have discovered that this is not an easy thing to do. To do so, you had to go through the displeasure, or pain, of making the change. If you have established a new habit, you did so by withstanding this pain until you discovered more pleasure from not smoking, in the form of praise from others, your pleasure

in spending less money, or a feeling of achievement.

And now we can return to our discussion of the roadblocks in the way of success. If you do not have habits that fit in with the type of success you desire, then you will have difficulty in achieving that success. In the rest of this book, I shall try to help you to become aware of how your present habits influence your efforts to succeed.

As a start, let's see if you can make a preliminary analysis of your habits, defining those which you think will help and those which will hinder your success in college. To help you to do this, I have given the analysis made by a representative college student whom we will call David. Figure 1 is made up of statements of the habits which David has listed for himself, either as aids or hindrances in his attempts to succeed. As we shall see later, when David's progress is used to illustrate other points, this initial analysis proves to be quite accurate.

At this time, notice that David has listed "I read slowly" as a habit that hinders his success; at the same time, he has listed "I check work carefully" as a helpful mental habit. As you study Figure 1, also notice that David has listed only a few habits. We shall

Figure 1 • DAVID'S ANALYSIS OF HIS HABITS

Habits Which Should Help College Success

Mental Habits
    I check work carefully
    I am very precise in my work
    I always complete tasks on time
Social Habits
    I am polite to others
    I listen to older people
Physical Habits
    I keep myself clean
    I do not smoke

Habits Which Should Hinder College Success

Mental Habits
    I read slowly
    I lose concentration easily
Social Habits
    I rarely join groups
Physical Habits
    I get tired easily

see later, in Chapter VI, that he can use other sources of information to discover some of his other habits.

List your own habits in Activity Sheet 1.[1] Later on you will probably be able to identify others, and you will have a chance to extend your list as part of your analysis in Chapter VI.

YOUR PRESENT ATTITUDES ARE IMPORTANT

Your attitudes represent another potential roadblock. In fact, they can be more damaging than habits because we are usually much less aware of our attitudes. Let's discuss what I mean by attitudes.

An attitude is a predisposition to behave in a certain way. For example, if you have a positive attitude toward honesty, you *will tend* to act in an honest way, regardless of the circumstances. This does not mean that you will always be honest, but rather that you have a strong tendency to be honest.

By contrast, if you have a negative attitude toward domineering people, you will tend to act negatively toward them. Thus, when you encounter a domineering teacher, you will tend to dislike him and to act contrary to his demands.

You have attitudes toward a great many things—people, ideas, conditions, objects, places, and so on. They develop as a result of your previous experiences, and, for the most part, *you learn your attitudes from other people without realizing it.* As a child you tended to adopt the attitudes of your parents, relatives, and close friends, because you probably thought highly of these people, and, without realizing it, you began to copy their ways of thinking and behaving. Sometimes the reverse occurs. Because a child may not get along well with these significant people,

he may develop *opposite* attitudes. Regardless of the direction, however, your parents, relatives, friends, and sometimes teachers influence the development of your attitudes.

Because this process occurs slowly, over a period of years, you are not normally aware of your attitudes or how they evolved. As with habits, you typically act without realizing that your attitudes are influencing you. This is one reason why it is so hard to *change* attitudes. However, if you can become clearly aware of your attitude toward something and see how it has developed, you will then be more able to change the attitude.

Let's return to our friend David. He was failing a history course. As we talked about this situation, David said he didn't know why he was failing; he felt that he was studying in this course as he had in other history courses. However, when he described his teacher, Mr. Johnson, it became clear that he had a negative attitude toward him. When I asked David how he felt toward Mr. Johnson, he said that he really hadn't given that much thought. After several minutes of discussion, however, David admitted that he didn't think much of him, "because he doesn't really know his subject. Instead of giving us lectures, he just talks with us about the subject. What kind of a teacher is that!"

David's reactions to Mr. Johnson seem based upon his negative attitude toward a certain type of teacher—the teacher who discusses. As we talked, David became aware of his attitude and added that he had always felt this way, although he really didn't know when or where he had developed this attitude toward "discussing" teachers.

Several weeks later, when David and I were talking again about his progress, he indicated that he had given some thought to his attitude toward Mr. Johnson. He was convinced that he had felt this way toward other "discussing" teachers. He then added that his mother also "dislikes teachers who waste time." As David and I talked more about this, he thought that perhaps he had learned his attitude from his mother. We then discussed

---

[1] This is the first of many Activity Sheets that appear at the end of this book. Studying these and filling them out for yourself will help you apply the ideas of this book to yourself.

the meaning of this negative attitude for his college achievement.

Some months later I saw David again. During this conference he noted that he had barely passed Mr. Johnson's course. "As a result of our discussions," he said, "I am now giving more thought to the type of teacher from whom I can learn."

David's experience points out that your success in college can be influenced by your attitudes, and it also illustrates that typically you do not see how this influence occurs. It further suggests that an awareness of your attitudes can be used to change them or to avoid situations where they will have a negative influence (David's behavior).

If you apply these ideas to yourself, it should be clear that your present attitudes may be a roadblock to success. Look at David's analysis of his attitudes in Figure 2, and carry out a similar analysis for yourself by completing Activity Sheet 2. The preliminary listing you develop now can be enlarged later, of course, but your present listing will be valuable as we discuss other possible roadblocks.

YOUR PERSONALITY NEEDS ARE IMPORTANT TOO

So far we have looked at habits and attitudes as potential roadblocks. Now we must look at something even more difficult to describe and understand—*personality needs.* They are more difficult to describe and understand because most people are unaware that they possess them. *Personality needs refer to those biological and psychological forces within the person that affect his behavior in their attempts to gain their own satisfactions.*

Let's look at this definition more closely. These forces refer to internal conditions that may or may not be in balance. If they are in balance (in a calm state), they are not affecting you directly. If they are not in balance (in an excited state), they are seeking to be satisfied; that is, they are attempting to return to a calm state. In this process, they have a direct and powerful effect on your behavior.

Several of these forces are aroused by a biological lack—a lack of food or water; several by bodily secretions and excretions—sex, lactation, urination, and defecation; several by avoidance conditions—heat avoidance and cold avoidance; several by a psychological lack—a lack of love, of achievement, of autonomy; and at least one by a striving toward the realization of one's inner potentialities—self-actualization. This means that personality needs are involved both in your basic efforts to survive as well as in your efforts to attain one of man's loftiest goals—complete self-fulfillment.

With such a variety of needs, it is not surprising to find that needs develop in several ways. The biologically based needs, of course, are very much influenced by heredity. Your strivings for food, water, urination, sex, and cold avoidance are dependent upon hereditary conditions, but even these biologically based needs are influenced by your experiences and learnings. However, other types of needs are primarily the result of environ-

Figure 2 • DAVID'S ANALYSIS OF HIS ATTITUDES

Positive
    I like most teachers
    I enjoy school most of the time
    I don't mind hard work
    I am willing to follow good leaders

Negative
    I dislike "talky" teachers
    I dislike non-practical school subjects
    I don't like rough sports

mental experiences and learnings, and, like habits and attitudes, they are also significantly affected by early family life.

The internal force exerted by a need, regardless of its type or how it evolved, affects your behavior. As a need becomes aroused, you behave in ways that you sense will satisfy it. Actually, you will typically have several needs that are not in balance at the same time. If these needs complement each other, your behavior will probably be smooth and satisfying. If they are in conflict, your behavior is likely to be disjointed and frustrating.

It is easy to understand why personality needs are so important. In addition to being a basic part of you, they indirectly or directly affect your behavior and thus influence your efforts to achieve success. In fact, in a very significant way, they affect the type of success you desire.

But this influence is rarely understood, because *often you are unaware of your personality needs.* This lack of awareness is even more pronounced than your unawareness of your habits and attitudes, probably because of your inability to pinpoint or identify the strivings or uneasiness you sometimes feel. Although you may know that you don't feel calm or satisfied with yourself, you can rarely say, "I now have a strong need for love," or "I am frustrated because I have a strong sex need," or "there is now a conflict between my need for achievement and my need for affiliation."

In addition, you seldom know how your personality needs have developed. This is especially true of achievement, autonomy, aggression, dominance, affiliation, and love, since it is most unlikely that you can trace their evolution from infancy. Even if you could, it would be difficult to change them although you might desire to do so. Because these needs are constantly influencing you, your behavior is directed at satisfying them, and you have to withstand considerable frustration of one or more needs while attempt-

ing to develop new or satisfy weaker ones. Thus, you tend to carry out behaviors to satisfy present needs, which in turn prevent the establishment of new ones.

What does all of this discussion mean to you and your desire to succeed in college? First, you should now realize that, because you are probably unaware of your personality needs, they can easily prevent you from obtaining the success you think you want. Even as you read this sentence, they are affecting you!

Second, although it is difficult to become aware of personality needs, some kinds of behavior suggest certain needs, and you can, with help, learn to observe your own behavior. You then may be able to change the type of success you desire or the behavior directed toward your goals. I shall develop this point in much more detail later, but, at this time, let me illustrate by referring again to our friend David.

Some time ago, when he came in to see me, he was having trouble with his course work. Particularly, he did not like the way his history teacher conducted his class. I have noted David's negative attitude toward "discussing" teachers. In addition to this attitude, David also displayed behaviors that represented certain personality needs. As we talked, he became aware of his strong needs for achievement, affiliation, conformity, and orderliness. In other words, he realized that he wanted to succeed to a great extent, but that he also wanted to be with people, to submit to their desires, and to have everything in "its right place."

You can probably see why David's personality needs posed some problems for him with his history professor. In effect, Mr. Johnson was requiring independence of thought, while David wanted to conform. Mr. Johnson taught in a "messy academic atmosphere," whereas David wanted a "neat and tidy" classroom. Thus, David's personality needs were inconsistent with Mr. Johnson's requirements. Recognizing his personality needs later helped David in his selection of other courses, since he could anticipate some of the problems he might have.

Although David's problem worked out fairly well, you cannot expect that your efforts to understand and deal with your needs will always be successful. One of my tasks during the following chapters will be to help you explore this area as much as possible, and later I shall ask you to list your own personality needs.

UNCONSCIOUS FACTORS INFLUENCE ALL OF US

In our discussions of habits, attitudes, and personality needs, I have pointed out that we are frequently unaware of our habits and attitudes and only very rarely aware of our personality needs; in other terms, we are not conscious of them. Thus, you may have a habit that you really do not know you have—perhaps you are unaware of your current reading habit. If this is so, we can say that your reading habit is an *unconscious factor to you.* On the other hand, you may be perfectly aware of this habit but unaware of how it affects your behavior. In this instance, your lack of awareness of its effects is the unconscious factor.

This is one way of looking at unconscious factors. But there is another way, more difficult to explain and understand: *we can also refer to unconscious factors as those thoughts and feelings that are in the unconscious part of your personality.* In this sense I am referring to personality as that whole which is made up of all of your characteristics as a person. One part of this totality incorporates those thoughts and feelings that lie below the surface, so that you yourself are not aware that they are part of your personality. Personality needs are typically "below the surface" and, thus, in the unconscious part of your personality.

In addition to needs, you probably also have certain thoughts and feelings that re-

main in your unconscious, because you would encounter too much pain if you allowed yourself to deal with them consciously. For example, most of us have, at one time or another, consciously thought of killing someone when we were very angry at that person. Since this thought has upset us greatly, we have typically "pushed it out of our minds." When we do this, the thought usually remains, but only in the unconscious part of our personality—it is an unconscious factor.

The same thing can happen with feelings. As a child you may have had very jealous feelings toward your brother. If you learned while growing up that jealousy was not an approved way of feeling, you probably "forgot" your jealousy. However, because you did so, the feeling probably remained in the unconscious part of your personality. If this was so, the feeling is there, but you are not aware of it!

There is still another way of viewing unconscious factors. This view of them has to do with the way that thoughts and feelings become unconscious. *Typically these thoughts and feelings are "forgotten" through an unconscious process.* This process involves your use of certain *defense mechanisms* that operate without your realizing it—that is, unconsciously. Defense mechanisms are the unconscious thought processes which you use to protect yourself from unpleasant thoughts and feelings; they include rationalization, projection, and compensation. Without going into an explanation of each of these mechanisms, it should be sufficient to note here that they are used by all of us, are learned behaviors, and help us live with ourselves. At the same time, though, you should not ignore their influence on your behavior. As part of your unconscious, they typically have a powerful effect on your efforts to succeed.

This is exactly why it is important that you understand that unconscious factors influence all of us. If you do not recognize that they are influencing you, they can become a great roadblock to your success, without your every knowing why you fail to succeed. You should also recognize that knowing you have unconscious factors does not automatically mean that you can understand them. On the contrary, you may never become *very* aware of these factors, although at times you can, on your own or with professional help, become more aware of your unconscious. Under these circumstances, you can then use what you know about your unconscious to help you succeed.

I shall describe in Chapters VI and VII how you can become somewhat aware of your unconscious. Since, at this time, you are probably unaware of your unconscious factors, you cannot yet list them as you did your habits and attitudes.

DEALING WITH THESE POTENTIAL ROADBLOCKS

I have pointed out and discussed with you four potential roadblocks: habits, attitudes, personality needs, and unconscious factors. And it should be clear to you that your efforts to succeed can be thwarted by any or all of these. Further, *it is not easy for any of us to deal with these potential roadblocks.* Thus,

it is very important that you take some precautions, so your efforts are not completely fruitless.

Fortunately, you have already taken one important step: by reading this chapter you are now aware of these conditions, and you can be on the alert for their possible influence. This is a necessary precaution: if you do not attempt to understand your own habits, attitudes, personality needs, and unconscious factors, or if you do not try to recognize their presence, then it is very likely that they will interfere with your efforts to succeed.

Later I shall discuss each of these factors in more detail, pointing out how you can become more aware of them, and suggesting some steps that you can take to help you modify them.

At this point, if you wish to know more about these concepts, you can either skip to later chapters or study some of the references which I have listed at the end of this chapter. You may also want to discuss these ideas with one of your teachers or your counselor. The latter can be especially helpful regarding your personality needs and unconscious factors.

THOUGHT QUESTIONS²

1. What habits do you have that should help you succeed in college?

2. How did you acquire these habits?

3. Which of your attitudes may hurt your efforts to succeed in college? Why?

4. Name at least three of your strong personality needs. How do you know you have these needs?

5. What precautions can *you* take to minimize the negative effects of your habits, attitudes, personality needs, and unconscious factors?

² At the end of each chapter I shall list questions that will help you relate the ideas in the chapter to yourself. Completing the Activity Sheets as you read each chapter should help you to answer these questions. Filling out the Activity Sheets *and* answering the questions should provide you with maximum benefits.

SELECTED REFERENCES

Habits

Coleman, J. C., and others. *Success in College*. Chicago: Scott Foresman, 1960. Chapter 3.

Farquhar, William, and others. *Learning to Study*. New York: Ronald Press, 1960. Chapters 1–3, 10.

Lass, Abraham H. *How to Prepare for College*. New York: David White Co., 1962. Chapter 7.

Morgan, Clifford T., and Deese, James. *How to Study*. New York: McGraw-Hill, 1957. Chapter 2.

Attitudes

Dudycha, George J. *Learn More with Less Effort*. New York: Harper, 1957. Chapter 7.

Fisher, M. B., and Noble, J. L. *College Education as Personal Development*. Englewood Cliffs: Prentice-Hall, 1960.

Garrison, Roger H. *The Adventure of Learning in College*. New York: Harper, 1959. Chapters 3, 5, 8, 10, 12.

Wilson, Eugene S., and Bucher, Charles A. *College Ahead!*, rev. ed. New York: Harcourt Brace, 1961. Chapter 10.

Personality Needs

Daly, Sheila J. *Questions Teen-Agers Ask*. New York: Dodd Mead, 1963. Chapters 9–10.

Heyns, Roger W. *The Psychology of Personal Adjustment*. New York: Dryden Press, 1958. Chapters 2–5.

Lazarus, Richard S. *Adjustment and Personality*. New York: McGraw-Hill, 1961. Chapter 2.

Lindgren, Henry C. *Psychology of Personal and Social Adjustment*, rev. ed. New York: American, 1959. Chapter 2.

Menninger, William C. *Growing Up Emotionally*. Chicago: Science Research Associates, 1960. Chapters 1–8.

Unconscious Factors

Heyns, Roger W. *The Psychology of Personal Adjustment*. New York: Dryden Press, 1958. Chapter 1, 4, 6.

Lindgren, Henry C. *Psychology of Personal and Social Adjustment*, rev. ed. New York: American, 1959. Chapter 1.

Combs, Arthur, and Snygg, Donald. *Individual Behavior*, rev. ed. New York: Harper, 1959. Chapters 7, 8.

Wattenberg, William W. *The Adolescent Years*. New York: Harcourt Brace, 1955. Chapter 24.

CHAPTER III

Your Reasons for Going to College Are Important

In the first chapter you found that you and your college are unique. Part of your uniqueness has to do with the particular kind of success you desire. You also know now that *you may not be able to understand fully what kind of success you desire, or how you are presently attempting to achieve that success.* The purpose of this chapter, then, is to help you discover what kind of success you *really* want. Further, I hope you will be able to discover the kind of success your college wants for you. A third goal is to help you see the implications of the similarities and differences between the success you desire and the success your college desires for you. Then, in Chapter IV, we will look at the abilities and the types of learning required by your college.

WHY ARE YOU GOING TO COLLEGE?

If you say you want to succeed in college, it is important that you know what you *really* mean by success. Even though you may think you know, I believe you will find it useful to complete Activity Sheet 3.

Let's assume that you are like many other students. If so, you probably have listed reasons such as earning a living, improving yourself socially, pressure from your parents, learning a profession or vocation, pressure from friends, acquiring knowledge, or finding a marriage partner as your reasons for attending college. For our purposes, it does not matter *what* you have listed. The important thing at this point is that you are honest with yourself as to why you are going to college. Your list is just as *good* as another student's list; it is good because it represents you. In this sense, it also represents your definition of success. In other words, *you now have on paper your real definition of success.*

On the other hand, if you have been unable to list any specific reasons why you are going to college, this suggests that you do not have a clear definition of success. It is extremely important that you recognize this fact, and, before going any further in this chapter, you should give additional thought to this problem. If, after you have thought about this for a while, you are still unable to list specific reasons why you are going to college, there are several steps you can take: you might talk to your school or college counselor, several friends, or your parents; also, you might want to read books and articles in which other college students discuss their reasons for attending college. To help you to do this, I have included in the list of references at the end of this chapter books by Heyns and Havighurst that should help.

Assuming that you now have a specific list of reasons why you are going to college, we can turn to an analysis of them. Stating it another way, we can classify the types of success you desire. In Chapter I, I indicated that students can be concerned primarily with academic, artistic, social, athletic, economic, or occupational success. Let's look at what these terms mean.

Academic success means that the individual desires a high scholastic average or a high level of scholastic learning (without necessarily obtaining high grades) or both. A student can obtain high grades without really learning much scholastically! Also, because there are many aspects of scholastic learning (for example, accumulation of in-

formation and critical thinking), a student has to know which of these aspects he desires.

Artistic success means that the individual desires to express himself through artistic means—through music, painting, sculpture, dancing, writing, drama, and so on. He recognizes his artistic success by his own feeling of satisfaction and the recognition he receives from other artists, experts, and the general public. Tangible recognition can be in the form of awards, grants, prizes, election to professional societies, or financial gain, but these tangible signs of success need not be present.

Social success means that the individual desires to be well accepted and to function well with others socially. He recognizes that he has achieved social success when he is accepted into groups of his own choosing (fraternity, club, informal clique, and so on) and when his behavior enables him to maintain his membership in these groups. Social success can also refer to boy-girl relations. When a boy or girl strives to meet, date, or marry his opposite number, these behaviors also are directed at social success. The person who is striving for social success of any kind is seeking achievement in interpersonal relations. He may seek these relationships for their own sake or because they lead to a better job, to increased wealth, and so on.

Athletic success means that the student desires to be an outstanding player in a sport. He recognizes success in this area by various conditions: team membership; awarding of letters or other symbols of achievement; recognition by peers, coaches, and the mass media.

Economic success means that the individual desires to earn or accumulate enough money to purchase the goods and services he desires. If a person is primarily concerned with economic success, he is not too worried about the manner by which he earns or accumulates his wealth: the main goal is to have the wealth. He recognizes this success by the amount of money he earns, the goods he can buy, and the services he can afford in comparison to the other members of his society.

Occupational success means that a person desires to gain a position and advance in the occupation of his choice, and it also implies that he is able to select, prepare for, and enter that occupation. The kind of occupation (professional, skilled, and so on) or the rewards (pay, security, and so on) may indicate success. Although the person probably takes these factors into consideration in selecting the occupation, they do not always determine if he is successful occupationally, since his success also depends on whether he stays in that occupation.

Now that we have examined each of these types of success, you should be aware of the fact that we may strive for more than one of these types. In fact, *some of us attempt to gain several types of success simultaneously.* You should also notice that we can be achieving several types of success while *consciously* striving for only one type. For example, although you are working toward occupational success, you may also be gaining academic success while you prepare for your occupation. Likewise, high achievement in your occupation may lead to economic success.

With this explanation of the types of success as a basis, let us now return to your analysis of your reasons for going to college. Complete Activity Sheets 4 and 5.

Since you have now identified the types of success that are most, least, and moderately important to you, we will pause here so that I can clarify my view of my role in helping you achieve the types of success you desire. I indicated in Chapter I that I would attempt in this book to help you succeed in college, but I will emphasize *one* type of success—the academic. Thus, *if your definition of success does not include academic success, you probably will not obtain much help from the rest of this book.* If your definition includes the academic (even if it is very low in your ratings), then you should benefit

from what follows. Indirectly, I hope you will also gain help in obtaining the other types of success you desire.

I must point out one more consideration before continuing. Although the rest of this book does not emphasize ideas related to non-academic success, you should not infer that these other types of success are not worthy! On the contrary, I believe that most students would be healthier if they could achieve several kinds of success. Accordingly, I have listed at the end of this chapter readings by Coleman and Dalton that should help you with the non-academic areas. In addition to reading these references, you might want to talk to your counselor, teachers, friends, and parents about these areas.

Let us now proceed with our discussion of your reasons for going to college. You have identified and classified types of success you desire. I'm sure you can understand that other students will rate *their* reasons differently. In fact, some students will desire different types of success, depending upon their specific reasons. Since this is so, we must ask this question: Are some types of success or reasons for wishing to succeed better than others?

Although this appears to be a simple question, its answer is very complex. We must first ask another question: Better for what and for whom? In other words, no one set of reasons is best for all students: the value of one's choice depends upon the particular student and the particular situation. This means that we cannot arbitrarily say that your reasons for going to college are "good" or "bad." If these reasons fit in well with your goals, habits, attitudes, personality needs, and unconscious factors, we can say that these are "good" reasons. They are "good" because they are consistent with the other aspects of your personality.

However, you should keep in mind that, if your list of reasons does not include ones related to academic success, you probably will not attain that type of success! In this case, we can say that you have "bad" reasons, if you are at all interested in graduating from your college. In other words, your stated goal —graduating from college—is inconsistent with your real reasons for going to college.

Perhaps you can now see that there is an important relationship between your real reasons for going to college and your behavior in college. *Your behavior is dependent upon these reasons, not upon what you would like your reasons to be or your stated goal.* Let's refer again to our friend David. In his own mind, David was attending college for several reasons, which included a desire to become an accountant, an interest in learning more about society, and a desire to learn how to get along with people better. As he discussed his goals with me, he realized that he was also influenced by the fact that all of his friends were going to college and by his parents' desire for him to go to college.

When David was having trouble with his history course, we analyzed the above-mentioned reasons at some length. As David talked about his second goal—an interest in learning more about society—he realized that this goal really did not mean much to him. Although he did want to learn more about people, he really didn't care about their past. He was more interested in why people act as they do. He wanted to understand the psychology of an individual's behavior.

With this new perception of his college goals, David was able to see more clearly why he was having trouble with his history course. Not only did he dislike the way his professor taught, but he really wasn't interested in the subject matter! Although this knowledge wasn't particularly helpful to him then, it did help him plan his course selections later. He made sure he included the introductory psychology course in his schedule.

David's experience clearly points out why it is extremely difficult to say that certain goals or types of success are better than any others. For David, his real goal of understanding human behavior was good. He would probably be able to achieve this type of goal; whereas he was unable to achieve the more globular one. The fact that he was able to identify his real reason meant that this reason was more likely to be appropriate for him.

But what about you? You have now identified your reasons for going to college. How can you discover if they are appropriate for you? Before attacking that question, we must look more carefully at your college. After all, if you are to achieve the success you have identified, you will need to do this either at your present or at some other college (assuming that you desire goals related to college work). Therefore, let us now turn to an analysis of why your college exists.

WHY DOES YOUR COLLEGE EXIST?

It may seem peculiar to you to say that a college can have reasons for existing. Perhaps you have always thought of a college as inanimate—something that just exists as a group of buildings someplace. More probably, you have realized that colleges differ from each other in certain ways (size of campus, fame of football teams, reputation for scholars, and so on). But have you ever realized that each college is like a human being in many ways? It has a distinct personality. This personality (its uniqueness) results from many things: its particular set of buildings, its set of academic regulations, its faculty members, its staff of specialists (counselors, physicians, dormitory directors, and so on), its historical background. All of these factors, and many more, influence its reasons for being.

In other words, each college has various reasons for existing, which are created, either deliberately or haphazardly, by the group of people who support, administrate, and teach in that college and which are influenced by the history of the institution. Since colleges differ in their particular reasons for existing (their goals or definitions of success), it benefits the student to know the reasons for his college's existence.

To help you obtain a better understanding of your college, complete Activity Sheet

6. If you are able to list more than five reasons, you probably have already been giving some thought to this question. If you have trouble listing five reasons, you may want to take some additional time to think about this before proceeding further. You might ask yourself if *your attitudes* toward doing this kind of thinking are interfering with your progress.

Assuming that you have been able to list at least five reasons for your college's existence, we are now ready to compare your list with the reasons stated by your college. A college usually indicates the reasons for its existence in several sources, such as the College Bulletin(s) and the Freshman Handbook. To illustrate this, I have listed in Figure 3, the reasons for the existence of the University of Rochester, as I have derived them from the first section of the Official Bulletin and the Freshman Handbook. Notice that several types of reasons are listed. One type refers to intellectual knowledge: the university seems very committed to discovering new knowledge, and it also wants its students to learn how to discover and use new knowledge. A second type of goal refers to the student's behavior: the university wants students to study independently and intensively various subjects, and it also encourages wide interests. The third type of goal is vocational: the university trys to prepare students for various professions and advanced research positions.

From this example, you should be ready to analyze your College Bulletin and Fresh-

man Handbook. Use Activity Sheet 7 for this analysis. After you have done so, notice the similarities and differences between *your* list of your college's goals (Activity Sheet 6) and the list for *your college* (Activity Sheet 7). If the two lists are quite similar, you can assume that you have a good picture of what your college desires to achieve. If, however, the two lists are quite different, this suggests that you do not understand what your college desires. In this case you must be very careful. It is extremely important that you understand what your college says it wants to achieve. If you do not understand what the stated goals mean, it would be helpful to discuss them now with one or more of your professors and with your advisor. Be careful! Are there any habits, attitudes, or unconscious factors affecting you that prevent you from doing this?

Assuming that you understand what your college's stated goals mean, we can now go further. *The stated reasons or goals represent your college's definition of success*, the types of success which your college seeks to attain. Now we can classify these reasons and compare them with your reasons for going to college. To do this, fill in Activity Sheets 8 and 9.

From this information you can now see the similarities and differences between the types of success you and your college desire. Note where they are the same. If you and your college agree on the most important type of success desired, your reasons for going to college *are appropriate to your college*. If

Figure 3 • GOALS OF THE UNIVERSITY OF ROCHESTER*

1. Interested in discovering the ways in which man's knowledge can be advanced.
2. Interested in applying these techniques to the important intellectual questions of our day.
3. Interested in teaching students the methods and fruits of this inquiry.
4. Believes that knowledge is important for mankind.
5. Believes students should have responsibility for independent study.
6. Encourages students to explore interests other than those of the major area of study.
7. Requires intensive study of each subject area.
8. Encourages students wanting high degree of intellectual challenge.
9. Prepares students for medical, nursing, musical, engineering, business, and teaching professions.
10. Prepares students for various research and professional careers requiring graduate study.

* Derived from an analysis of the College Bulletin and the Freshman Handbook.

you and your college also agree on the moderately important types of success desired, this is another positive point.

Now we can go back to a question we looked at before: Are your identified reasons for going to college apporpriate to you? We have determined part of the answer to this question. *If you and your college are striving for "most" and "moderately" important types of success that are similar, you have some evidence that your reasons are appropriate, or "good," for you.*

By contrast, you can see that if you and your college are *not* striving for the same types of success, there are several problems. It may be that your reasons are *inappropriate*, insofar as they are able to prevent you from achieving success in your college, because they are not consistent with the kinds of success for which your college is striving. Or it may be that your reasons are *appropriate for another college.* If your reasons do agree with those of a different college, you will probably have a greater chance of succeeding in that college. Thus, your present reasons would be appropriate if you were attending that college!

I have just pointed out one very practical consideration concerning the comparison of your definition of success and that of your college's. If they agree, you can assume that you should continue to attend your college. If they *disagree,* however, you may have to change colleges. Of course, another solution is possible: you can change your definition of success!

This sounds easy enough, but watch out! At this point your prior habits, attitudes, personality needs, and unconscious factors can prevent you from doing something you would consciously like to do. Before looking at this problem further, however, we need to look at your college's definition of success in more detail and to examine your definition of success in more depth also. Then you will be able to determine with more assurance that your reasons for going to college are really appropriate, or inappropriate, for you.

YOUR COURSES HAVE CERTAIN REASONS FOR EXISTING TOO

In the above section we have seen that each college has certain reasons for existing. As you identified your college's reasons or goals, you have probably noticed that these are stated in general terms. They do not spell out in any detail what the student should achieve. At the same time, however, you must realize that academic success in most colleges depends upon the student's achievement in specific courses. This means the student must meet the definition of success that exists for each course. Each course, in its own way, adds a bit to the definition of success of the whole college. Thus, if a student succeeds in the various courses he takes, he succeeds in that college.

Determining the goals of each course is not easy. However, there are several things that can be done to facilitate this process. The description of a course in the College Bulletin should describe, in general, what the course is striving to achieve. Reading the syllabus or outline of a course and talking to the instructor should also help. Finally, talking to several students who have taken the same course from the same teacher can give additional information.

To help you understand the nature of course goals, I have developed a list of goals for Psychology 20 and listed them in Figure 4.[1] You should notice that a variety of goals exist and that the instructor for the course and his students do *not* view the course in the same way. Thus, it is difficult for a student to determine all the goals of a course by speaking only to other students who have taken it. Now, you can determine the goals for one of your present courses, using Activity Sheet 10 for this purpose.

You should now be in a better position to determine the goals of all the courses you

---

[1] Although Psychology 20 is a fictitious course, the information presented here is representative of many introductory college psychology courses.

Figure 4 • GOALS OF PSYCHOLOGY 20

---

1. *List of goals from College Bulletin:*
    To help student survey the whole field of psychology.
    To have student know the basic facts related to human behavior.
    To help student appreciate the importance of psychology.
2. *List of goals from syllabus or outline:*
    Neither syllabus nor outline contain information about goals.
3. *List of goals from discussion with instructor:*
    To get student to remember established psychological facts.
    To have student use scientific method in studying human behavior.
    To have student understand the ways that psychology can be used in different occupations.
4. *List of goals from discussion with students:*
    To have student memorize detailed facts from the textbook.
5. *Composite list of course goals from all sources:*
    To help student survey the whole field of psychology.
    To have student remember established facts in psychology (from text especially).
    To have student understand how psychology is important in our lives and in different occupations.
    To have student use scientific method in studying human behavior.

---

are taking. Use Activity Sheet 11 for this purpose. Once you have done this, you can return to the overall problem we were looking at before: Do you have appropriate reasons for going to college?

Assuming that you have now completed listing your goals for all of your current courses, let us compare them to your reasons for going to college. Use Activity Sheet 12 to make this comparison. This listing should tell you something more about your chances of achieving the type of success you desire. We have already compared your reasons with the goals for the entire college. Now you can compare your goals with the goals of the particular courses in which you are trying to succeed. *Where your reasons and your courses' goals are similar, you can say that your reasons are appropriate for these particular courses.* Where they are quite different, you can infer the opposite.

Before concluding that your reasons are inappropriate, however, remember that we are talking about your efforts to succeed in a particular college and in particular courses. As I have mentioned earlier, your reasons may be more appropriate in a different college; they may also be more appropriate to different courses.

Thus, we once again come to the problem of what you can do if your reasons or goals are different from those of your college and

your courses. One obvious answer is to change colleges. Another is to change courses or curricula. If your goals are more in line with other courses or curricula, such a change should aid your efforts to succeed. If you think this solution is appropriate for you, this is a good time for discussing this situation with your advisor or counselor.

I have indicated earlier that another possible solution is to change your reasons for going to college (your definition of success), but that this is not an easy thing to do. You are well aware now that your habits, attitudes, personality needs, and unconscious factors may prevent a change of goals. If you would seriously like to change your reasons for wishing to succeed in college, however, some involved discussions with your advisor or counselor would be most beneficial. Likewise, it may prove valuable to talk with students whose goals are different from your own. In either case, do not be surprised if you find changing your goals a difficult and a long process. To help you in this effort, I have included at the end of this chapter references by Coleman, Heyns, Packard, and Wattenberg, and I also suggest that you discuss this problem with your counselor too. If you are anxious to know more about changing goals now, you might skip ahead to Chapter IX where I deal with this topic in more detail.

BY WAY OF SUMMARY

In this chapter we looked first at your reasons for going to college. I have indicated that these reasons or goals represent the kind of success you desire. As a result of carrying out several analytical steps, you should now have a better understanding of yourself than you did before reading this chapter. Further, we have looked more carefully at your college. Following your analysis of your college's statements of its goals, you should have more insight into why your college exists. Because we have also looked at specific courses and their reasons for being offered, you should have an even more realistic estimate of the kind of success your college wants you to achieve.

Finally, I have pointed out to you the implications of the above analyses. If your reasons for going to college are the same as your college's reasons for existing, you have increased your chances of succeeding. If they are different, however, your chances of succeeding are diminished, and we have discussed possible ways of dealing with this situation.

THOUGHT QUESTIONS

1. List the three most important reasons why you are attending college. What is your opinion of these reasons?
2. In what ways do you think your habits, attitudes, personality needs, and unconscious factors have influenced your reasons for going to college?
3. What reactions do you have to the goals of your college? Why do you react this way?
4. Do you like the goals of your current courses? To what extent are your reasons for going to college similar to the goals of your courses?
5. If your reasons for going to college and the goals of your courses differ, what should you do about this? What will you do?

SELECTED REFERENCES

Why Students Go to College

Coleman, J. C., and others. *Success in College.* Chicago: Scott Foresman, 1960. Chapter 2.

Dalton, Charles R. *College for You?* New York: Keystone, 1959. Chapters 1, 2, 4.

Farquhar, William, and others. *Learning to Study.* New York: Ronald Press, 1960. Chapter 1.

Garrison, Roger H. *The Adventure of Learning in College.* New York: Harper, 1959. Chapter 2.

Havighurst, Robert J., and Diamond, Esther E. *Should You Go to College?* Chicago: Science Research Associates, 1961. Chapters 1–9.

Heyns, Roger W. *The Psychology of Personal Adjustment.* New York: Dryden Press, 1958. Chapter 13.

Kalish, R. A. *Making the Most of College.* San Francisco: Wadsworth, 1959.

Morgan, Clifford T., and Deese, James. *How to Study.* New York: McGraw-Hill, 1957. Chapter 1.

Plummer, Robert H. *College Careers and You.* Chicago: Science Research Associates, 1963. Chapter 1–5.

Wilson, Eugene S., and Bucher, Charles A. *College Ahead!,* rev. ed. New York: Harcourt Brace, 1961. Chapter 7.

Achieving Non-Academic Success

Coleman, J. C., and others. *Success in College.* Chicago: Scott Foresman, 1960. Chapter 10, 11, 12, pp. 233–235.

Fisher, M. B., and Noble, J. L. *College Education as Personal Development.* Englewood Cliffs: Prentice-Hall, 1960.

Landis, Judson, and Landis, Mary. *Teenagers' Guide for Learning.* Englewood Cliffs: Prentice-Hall, 1957. Chapters 21, 22.

Ways of Changing Goals

Boone, Pat. *Between You, Me and the Gatepost.* Englewood Cliffs: Prentice-Hall, 1960. Chapters 1, 2, 3, 8.

Coleman, J. C., and others. *Success in College.* Chicago: Scott Foresman, 1960. Chapter 8, pp. 233–235.

Garrison, Roger H. *The Adventure of Learning in College.* New York: Harper, 1959. Chapters 4, 12, 13.

Heyns, Roger W. *The Psychology of Personal Adjustment.* New York: Dryden Press, 1958. Chapter 15.

Packard, Vance. *Do Your Dreams Match Your Talents?* Chicago: Science Research Associates, 1960. Chapters 1–8.

Townsend, Agatha. *College Freshmen Speak Out.* New York: Harper, 1956. Chapter 7.

Wattenberg, William W. *The Adolescent Years.* New York: Harcourt Brace, 1955. Chapters 2, 16.

CHAPTER IV

Your College Requires Certain Abilities and Types of Learning

IN THE PREVIOUS CHAPTER WE COMPARED YOUR reasons for going to college and your college's reasons for existing. This comparison of goals should have helped you to determine your chances of succeeding in your college. Further, I hope you have obtained some insights into how you can change your present behavior so as to obtain the success you desire.

It is foolish, however, to assume that success will automatically follow, once you and your college agree on the type of success that is important. As crucial as this is, obtaining any type of success also depends on other factors. In the academic area, two crucial ones are *abilities* and *types of learning*. In

this chapter, I shall discuss with you the nature of abilities and the kinds of abilities you possess and use and compare these with the kinds of abilities required by your college. Following this, we shall turn to the types of learning that can be used, the types required by your college, and the types you prefer and use best. Finally, we shall try to determine the meaning for you of the types of abilities and learning required by your college.

THE NATURE OF ABILITIES

Before we can discuss the abilities which you possess or which are required by colleges, I must explain what I mean by ability (or skill). *If you possess an ability this means you can perform a certain action or behavior, because of genetic inheritance and/or some previous learning.*

Let me spell out what this definition means. Each of us carries out various behaviors during the course of a day. If carrying out a specific behavior is dependent upon your biological inheritance from your parents and/or your past experiences, then we can say that behavior depends upon your ability to carry out that behavior. For example, you are now reading this sentence. This behavior is dependent upon your inheritance of certain biological body structures—such as the eye retina—and upon your past experiences in learning to read. Thus, reading that sentence was possible because you *possess* the ability to read. *Notice that ability refers to the current situation.* In contrast, the capacity or aptitude to do something refers to your *potential* to carry out a certain action or behavior in the *future*.

Also, there are various types of abilities. Some abilities involve simple behaviors while others involve a complex series of behaviors. The ability to sit up, for example, is much simpler than the ability to swim.

Likewise, abilities can be classified as essentially *mental*, *physical*, or *social* abilities. Mental abilities are those which are primarily dependent upon the functioning of the mind: examples are the ability to read, to think critically, to add numbers, to remember past events, and so on. Physical abilities are primarily dependent upon the functioning of the body: examples are the ability to walk, to eat, to run, to swim, to climb, and so on. Social abilities are those which are primarily dependent upon the functioning of one's personality in interpersonal situations. Examples are the ability to make friends, to live with a marriage partner, to participate in a fraternity meeting, to get along with older people, and so on.

Although abilities can be grouped into three classes, the examples given should indicate that most abilities require a combination of mental, physical, and/or social behaviors. Thus, the ability to swim, even though it is classified as essentially physical, usually requires the use of the mind. Likewise, the ability to make friends, essentially a social ability, usually involves the use of the mind too. Some abilities, such as the ability to paint, require an almost equal balance of mental and physical types of behavior.

YOU POSSESS CERTAIN ABILITIES

We can now turn to identifying the different kinds of abilities you possess and pick out those that are high and low for you. Various sources of information will help you to make this analysis. Your *high school record* should be especially fruitful, since it shows your progress over an extended period of time. It should include all facets of your high school experience. It should indicate the areas of academic achievement (and lack of achievement) and, thus, suggest where you have high mental abilities. It should also state your participation in extra-curricular activities and, thus, suggest the areas of non-academic achievement which, in turn, can suggest where you have high (or low) physical and social abilities.

You can use your *non-school activities* in the same way. By non-school activities, I am referring to situations such as your home, social clubs, service organizations, informal peer groups, and religious groups. By looking at your participation (or lack of participation) in such groups, you will be able to identify the kinds of mental, physical, and social abilities you have used in these situations. Incidentally, it should not surprise you to discover that you use somewhat different abilities in your school and non-school activities.

In addition to these two major sources of comprehensive information about your abilities, you can also use a more limited, but significant, source of information. You may have already taken some *ability or achievement tests* in high school or in college. These tests can indicate your highest and lowest abilities (typically *only* in the area of mental ability), as compared to the abilities of other students such as yourself. These tests supply more limited information because the results give only a sample of your abilities, rather than a complete picture over an extended period of time, such as your records of school and non-school activities give. Despite this shortcoming, results from these tests are valuable because you can use them to compare yourself with a student population much bigger and more diverse than that of your own high school or college. Thus, you can identify your highest and lowest mental abilities in comparison with thousands of students.

You should also use another source of information to supplement your records and test information. The *subjective observations* of your teachers, counselors, principal, group leader, or religious leader will tell you how other significant people view your abilities. They can point out to you how the "outside world" sees you. Because their perceptions may be quite different from your own, they should be considered before you conclude your analysis of your abilities.

Before proceeding with your own analysis, you might look at how David attempted to do this when he was a freshman in college. As he thought about his high school record, he came up with the summary listed in Figure 5.

David's information suggested that he was weak in the creative area of mental abilities, lacked physical stamina and coordination, and functioned best socially with close friends and in formalized social situations. Let's see if these observations hold up for his non-school activities which are listed in Figure 6.

Figure 5 • DAVID'S SUMMARY OF HIS HIGH SCHOOL RECORD

Highest Abilities	Lowest Abilities
Mental 1. Remembering facts 2. Answering specific textbook questions 3. Looking up information 4. Answering questions in class	*Mental* 1. Solving mathematical problems 2. Creating poetry 3. Using chemical equations
Physical 1. Running on track team	*Physical* 1. Playing team sports 2. Achieving coordination in shop courses 3. Completing physical fitness tests
Social 1. Getting along with a few good friends 2. Taking part in student council 3. Taking part in class committee meetings	*Social* 1. Making new friends 2. Joining a fraternity

Figure 6 • DAVID'S SUMMARY OF HIS NON-SCHOOL ACTIVITIES

Highest Abilities	Lowest Abilities
Mental 1. Passed Boy Scout merit badge tests 2. Remembered church regulations for confirmation 3. Passed driver's written test	*Mental* 1. Don't do crossword puzzles too well 2. Always get beaten in chess and checkers
Physical 1. Passed Boy Scout endurance hike tests	*Physical* 1. Avoid playing contact sports with friends 2. Not very handy with tools at home
Social 1. Enjoy having friends at home 2. Got along well with Boy Scout troop 3. Get along well with adults	*Social* 1. Have hard time getting dates 2. Find it hard to make new friends 3. Didn't do well in part-time selling job

His non-school activities tend to confirm the observations drawn from his school record. In addition, we also see that David's weakness in the area of social ability also applied to his ability to get dates and to succeed in his part-time job. When David went to talk to his high school counselor, he came up with a summary of the results of his ability and achievement tests which is listed in Figure 7. The test results again seem to confirm David's high school record. His ability tests suggest that his weakest area was in developing new ideas or seeing things differently (space relations and abstract reasoning require this). His achievement tests, however, do not give us any new information, except that they again point out that David had less ability in mathematics than in language.

After David talked to his counselor, he also conferred with several of his teachers, his Boy Scout leader, and his minister. David discovered that all of these people tended to view him in the same way: they saw him as a serious, highly motivated boy who did best when he had specific things to learn. They also mentioned that he seemed to like being with people but wasn't too good at meeting and socializing with new people. His physical education teacher also pointed out that he was below average in physical stamina and ability.

We can see, then, that these people also supported David's picture of his abilities. Using all of this information, David began to realize which of his mental, physical, and social abilities were strong and which were weak. This information allowed him to understand better the degree of success which he had achieved in college up to that point.

With this example in mind, you can proceed with your analysis of your own abilities. Perhaps you should start by again referring to some of the roadblocks that could prevent you from accomplishing this. You can see, by now, that your attitudes toward making this kind of analysis may prevent you from accomplishing it. Further, I'm sure you can understand that your personality needs can also block such an analysis, even though you would consciously like to achieve this goal. Probably the only thing you can do at this point is simply to realize that this may occur, and, if it does, perhaps then your college counselor will be able to help you.

Keeping this precaution in mind, carry out your analysis of your mental, physical, and social abilities. If, at this point, you believe you need a more thorough understanding of abilities, you can skip to Chapters X, XI, and XII, where crucial mental abilities are identified and discussed more completely. If you believe you are ready now, proceed by completing Activity Sheets 13–17.

After finishing this analysis, you probably have a more accurate and comprehensive picture of your abilities. However, you may feel that you really do not possess enough information to draw any meaningful conclusions. If this is the case, or if you believe that you have changed quite a bit since your high school days, you can still obtain additional information, by conferring with your college advisor or your college counselor, or by seeking out an educational and vocational counseling service.

Figure 7 • DAVID'S SUMMARY OF HIS ABILITY AND ACHIEVEMENT TEST RESULTS

Highest Mental Abilities	*Lowest Mental Abilities*

Ability Tests
  1. Numerical
  2. Language
  3. Clerical
	Ability Tests
	  1. Spatial relations
	  2. Mechanical
	  3. Abstract reasoning

Achievement Tests
  1. Social studies
  2. Language usage
	Achievement Tests
	  1. Mathematics

YOUR COLLEGE REQUIRES CERTAIN ABILITIES

Knowing about your abilities is good, but in itself it will probably not help you too much to increase your chances of succeeding in your college. You must now try to compare your abilities with those required by your college. In view of your analysis of your college's goals (Chapter III), it should not surprise you that your college may require somewhat different abilities from some other colleges. This is another aspect of your college's uniqueness. Your problem now is to discover the particular abilities that are required at your college. Once you have done this, you can then compare these requirements with the abilities you possess.

One way of determining these required abilities is to refer to the college and course goals you identified in Chapter III. From that information you can infer the types of mental, physical, and social abilities your college requires. Before you do this, let's use the examples from Chapter III to point out how you can make these inferences. We shall look at the general goals of the college first. You recall that I used as an example the goals of the University of Rochester, which I had derived from the College Bulletin and Freshman Handbook. From this list, I have now determined that the University of Rochester stresses the abilities listed in Figure 8.

Notice that I have rephrased the statements of the reasons for the university's existence (college goals), so that they point to specific abilities. Thus, the university's interest in teaching students the methods and fruits of intellectual inquiry (Reason 1), is stated as two mental abilities: Mental Abilities 1 and 2. Likewise, Reason 9 (Prepares students for medical, nursing, musical, engineering, business, and teaching professions) has been expressed as one mental, one physical, and one social ability. You should also notice that the university's goals require many types of mental abilities, but only one type of physical and one type of social ability. If I had used another college as an example, it is possible that additional types of physical and social abilities would have been required.

A more comprehensive listing of required abilities could be determined by analyzing the goals of the courses too, since they are derived not only from written statements, but also from discussions with faculty and students. Using your lists of the goals of your college and of your courses, therefore, can help you determine the abilities required at your college. Use Activity Sheets 18–20 for this purpose.

This information should make it possible for you to obtain some insight into your chances of succeeding in your college, and further, it should point out the areas which you need to concentrate on, if you are to increase your chances of succeeding. You can determine this by carrying out one more analysis: you must compare your highest abilities with those required at your college. To do this, complete Activity Sheet 21.

If this information shows that you possess the abilities required by your college,

Figure 8 • ABILITIES REQUIRED AT THE UNIVERSITY OF ROCHESTER

Mental
  1. Ability to remember methods of discovering new knowledge
  2. Ability to remember intellectual knowledge
  3. Ability to study independently
  4. Ability to develop interests in subjects other than those of the major area of study
  5. Ability to study intensively each subject area
  6. Ability to learn knowledge and skills required in chosen profession or research career

Physical
  1. Ability to use body (hand-eye coordination, etc.) when learning professional and research career skills

Social
  1. Ability to use the human relations skills required in the practice of a professional career

you can conclude that your chances of succeeding are quite good. However, if you do not have a sizable number of these required abilities, you should assume the opposite. This conclusion, however, may be subject to change, depending upon the type of abilities which you lack. If the abilities which you lack are, for the most part, genetically determined and physically based abilities (such as the abilities required in painting, playing a musical instrument, and playing football) or highly abstract mental abilities (such as the ability to handle advanced mathematical concepts, philosophical logic, and advanced psychological theory), there is not much you can do to improve your chances of succeeding. If the abilities which you lack are primarily dependent upon prior learning, however (such as basic reading, writing, or speaking), it is possible to increase your chances of succeeding. Although this may not be an easy task, with help and effort you can increase your proficiency in these types of abilities. I shall have much more to say about this in Chapters X, XI, and XII where I shall talk about modifying abilities.

YOUR COLLEGE ALSO REQUIRES CERTAIN TYPES OF LEARNING

Now we must look at the types of learning that your college requires. As we shall see, there is a close connection between the abilities you possess and the types of learning you prefer and can do best. *By learning, I'm referring to the process of changing your behavior; we can say that learning has occurred if behavior is changed as a result of some experience and not because of normal, physical growth.*

Let us start by discussing the types of learning that human beings use. Then you can see if your college tends to require some of these more than others. Following that, you can determine the types of learning you tend to prefer and use well, and finally you can see the importance of the kinds of learning you prefer for your chances of succeeding.

We can identify five kinds of learning that we typically use. Although we may not be conscious that we use each of these types, most people have used them at some point in their lives. The first, *trial and error*, is probably the most common way to learn. This means that behavior changes because the individual tries to do something, makes errors, and finally—practically by accident—finds a solution. In illustration, let's look at Mr. Jones, who doesn't know what size of hat he wears. In order to find out, he goes into a haberdashery and proceeds to try on every hat available. As soon as he tries on a hat which doesn't fit (tries and errs), he moves on to another hat. Suddenly, he finds one that fits perfectly. He looks at the label to see the hat size; he says to himself, "Ah, it's a 6⅜; my hat size is 6⅜." If Mr. Jones remembers his hat size when he goes to buy a hat later, we can conclude that he has learned it by trial and error.

The second type of learning, *rote*, is also very widely used, especially by students. In rote learning, the person attempts to remember something by repeating and repeating it until he has it firmly memorized, so that he can recall it without difficulty. Mr. Jones can try to remember his hat size by repeating to himself, over and over again, the following: "My hat size is 6⅜, 6⅜, 6⅜. My hat size is 6⅜, 6⅜, 6⅜," etc. After perhaps ten times he can then remember his hat size, and if he is able to remember it later on, we say he has learned it by rote.

The third type of learning is called *association*. In learning by association, something new is remembered by being associated with something that is already remembered. Thus, we learn something new by connecting it with something we have already learned. The past learning may be facts, principles, laws, and so on; this past learning serves as a foundation to which the new piece of information is added. In school situations, this foundation may be previous course material. In the case of Mr. Jones, it may be some indirect piece of information. For example, suppose his telephone number ends in "638"; by associating his telephone number, HA 6-5638, which he already knows, with his hat size, 6⅜, he can remember his hat size. Once again, if he is then able to remember this later on, we can say he has learned it by association.

The fourth type of learning is called *conscious problem-solving.* This means the individual learns by deliberately following a plan of action in order to solve a problem. In contrast to learning by trial and error, conscious problem-solving demands that the individual think up a way of trying to solve the problem before he actually tries any solutions. Because his plan of action is based upon previous learning, it produces much quicker learning. Let us use Mr. Jones as our example once more. Again he does not know his hat size. As he thinks about this problem, he remembers that haberdasheries have head measures that determine hat sizes. Therefore, he goes to the local haberdashery, asks the salesman to measure his head, and finds that his hat size is 6⅜. If Mr. Jones then remembers this information in the future, we can conclude that he has learned by conscious problem-solving.

The fifth type of learning is more difficult to explain and to illustrate than the previous four. *Unconscious insight* is quite different from any of the other methods of learning. Learning occurs in this instance even though the individual is not consciously trying to solve a problem or learn something. On the contrary, he may suddenly discover a solution to a problem he had been trying to solve for a long period of time but had set aside. Without even thinking about the problem or trying to remember it, he gets an insight, and suddenly, he has no trouble at all in solving or remembering it.

Again let's use Mr. Jones as our example. Assuming again that he does not know his hat size but that he wants to learn it, we note that he goes to a haberdashery and begins to try on various hats. Instead of finding the size by accident, as he did in our first example, he ends up without finding out his hat size at all. He leaves the store and thinks about his problem, but no matter how hard he tries, he cannot think of another way to solve his problem. Later in the day, while eating supper and not thinking about the problem of his hat size at all, he suddenly gets an idea. "Why not ask the salesman to measure my head," he thinks to himself. He feels great; he jumps out of his seat and rushes to the store, asks the salesman to measure his head, and finds that his hat size is 6⅜.

As the above examples indicate, many times we use several types of learning almost simultaneously. A person may use learning by association and rote for better memory; frequently, conscious problem-solving is followed by unconscious insight. When these combinations are used, better learning typically results.

With this explanation of the types of learning as background, you can now turn to analyzing the types of learning required at your college. Probably the best way of determining this is to look at the specific course goals and the required abilities that you have already identified. From these you can infer which types of learning are stressed at your college.

To help you do this, I shall first illustrate this procedure. Let's start by referring to the specific course goals. I identified the course goals for Psychology 20 and listed these in Chapter III; then, using this list, I looked to see which of the five types of learning were required to achieve each goal, by comparing the statement of the goal with the nature of each type of learning discussed above. I then filled in Figure 9.

Each X indicates the type of learning that will probably best achieve each goal. Thus, you will probably remember the established facts in psychology best by using rote

Figure 9 • TYPES OF LEARNING INFERRED FROM THE GOALS OF PSYCHOLOGY 20

Goals of Psychology 20	Types of Learning				
	Trial and Error	Rote	Association	Conscious Problem-Solving	Unconscious Insight
1. To give student survey of psychology		X	X		
2. To get student to remember facts		X	X		
3. To have student understand importance of psychology in everyday lives		X	X		
4. To have student use scientific method		X	X	X	X

and association learning. Likewise, to achieve the goal of using the scientific method to study human behavior, learning by rote, association, conscious problem-solving, and unconscious insight will probably be required. The two latter types of learning will be required in this case, because you will have to *use* the scientific method as opposed simply to *remembering* facts. To test your ability to use the scientific method, you will probably be given problems to solve.

You should note two other points about Figure 9. First, no checks are made in the trial and error column, not, however, because you cannot accomplish these goals by using trial and error, but rather, because better learning will result if you use rote and association. Second, the goals of Psychology 20 can best be achieved by using primarily two types of learning. However, if you rely only on rote and association, you will probably not

be completely successful; you will also have to use conscious problem-solving and unconscious insight.

To illustrate further, let's look at the freshman English course. The goals for this course in one particular college are to have the student:

1. understand the various forms and styles of writing;
2. analyze the form and style of writing of various pieces of literature;
3. express himself in writing with clarity and precision.

These goals require the types of learning listed in Figure 10. Because these goals are quite different from those of Psychology 20, there is considerable difference in the types of learning emphasized; here much more reliance is placed upon conscious problem-solving and unconscious insight. To be able to analyze a piece of literature requires an un-

Figure 10 • TYPES OF LEARNING INFERRED FROM THE GOALS OF A FRESHMAN ENGLISH COURSE

Goals of This Freshman English Course	Types of Learning				
	Trial and Error	Rote	Association	Conscious Problem-Solving	Unconscious Insight
1. Understanding of form and style		X	X	X	X
2. Analysis of form and style of literature				X	X
3. Ability to express one's self in writing with clarity and precision				X	X

derstanding of form and style and an application of this understanding to a particular piece of literature or a "problem." This is why conscious problem-solving and unconscious insight are required. Likewise, to express yourself in writing you must apply methods of writing which you have already learned to particular topics or "problems." In this sense, previous learning in terms of writing ability must now be applied to a new situation.

You should be ready at this point to turn to the course goals you have identified and to figure out the types of learning which are required. Use Activity Sheet 22 to accomplish this. To substantiate this information, you will need to analyze the abilities required

by your college and infer the types of learning from these.

For example, I have used the list of abilities required at the University of Rochester, as stated in Figure 8, and for each ability I have checked the types of learning most closely associated with it. Figure 11 contains this analysis.

Notice several points about this information. First, learning by association and conscious problem-solving are most frequently required at the University of Rochester. Second, learning by trial and error is least demanded. Note, however, that trial and error is valuable for developing new interests outside of the student's major area of study, developing body coordination, and developing hu-

Figure 11 • TYPES OF LEARNING INFERRED FROM REQUIRED ABILITIES AT THE UNIVERSITY OF ROCHESTER

Required Abilities	Types of Learning				
	Trial and Error	Rote	Association	Conscious Problem-Solving	Unconscious Insight
Mental					
1. Ability to remember methods of discovering new knowledge		X	X	X	
2. Ability to remember intellectual knowledge		X	X	X	
3. Ability to study independently		X	X	X	X
4. Ability to develop interests in subjects other than those of the major area of study	X		X	X	X
5. Ability to study intensively each subject area			X	X	X
6. Ability to learn knowledge and skills required in chosen profession or research career		X	X	X	X
Physical					
1. Ability to use body (hand-eye coordination, etc.) when learning professional and research career skills	X	X	X	X	X
Social					
1. Ability to use human relations skills required in the practice of a professional career	X	X	X	X	X

man relations skills. Third, rote learning is required to carry out physical and social abilities as well as mental abilities: the repetitious practice of body coordination movements and human relations skills. Fourth, unconscious insight is required in developing each of the three types of abilities, but it is not demanded for remembering methods of discovering new knowledge or for remembering intellectual knowledge. Thus, a student attending the University of Rochester would have to use all of the types of learning; to gain maximum success, however, he would have to apply each type to the appropriate kind of mental, physical, or social ability required.

We can now look at your own college. You have already identified the abilities required and should, thus, be able to identify the types of learning associated with each. Use Activity Sheet 23 for this purpose. Following this you can identify the types of learning required "frequently," "moderately," and "least" at your college. Completing Activity Sheet 24 will give you this information. Although these data are very important, before you can estimate their real significance you must determine the types of learning you prefer and can use well. This additional step will give you further evidence about your chances of succeeding in your college.

YOU PREFER AND USE WELL CERTAIN TYPES OF LEARNING

Now that you realize that your college requires some types of learning more than others, it should not surprise you to learn that you prefer some over others. Likewise, I'm sure that by this time you suspect that you can do better in some than others. Our task is to determine which of these types of learning you prefer and can use best.

There are several ways to determine your preferences. The first is *the way you study*. If you think about the typical procedures you use while studying, you should be able to estimate how much you use each of the various types of learning. For example, when you study assigned material, do you spend most of your time reading the assignment and then repeating to yourself the content of the material? If you do this, you are relying heavily on rote. On the other hand, if you ask yourself questions or use the author's questions about the material *before* you read it, you are relying on conscious problem-solving. You are using association if you try to connect the new material you have read with other course material or book material that you have previously learned.

A second source of evidence is your *reactions to certain courses*. As we have seen already, courses differ in their emphasis on the different types of learning. You probably react more favorably to those courses that emphasize the types of learning you prefer. Therefore, identify the courses you like or have liked in the past, and then see if you can determine the types of learning stressed in them. For example, you may like natural science (biology, chemistry, physics) and mathematics, all of which stress problem-solving. Since various teachers approach these courses differently, however, you cannot conclude that they will always emphasize problem-solving. On the contrary, it is quite possible that your former teachers in these courses have stressed rote learning. Nevertheless, if you can discover the courses you like, you probably will discover the types of learning preferred by the instructors. This should indirectly tell you about your preferences too.

A third source of information concerns your *non-school learnings*. You have learned new ideas, skills, and attitudes at home, in church, in clubs, and at camp. If you look at the typical ways you have approached these tasks, you can discover your preference for types of learning in these circumstances. For example, you may discover that you have relied heavily upon trial and error in these informal situations, whereas in school you have preferred association. If so, this is important to know.

In view of this discussion, you should be able to look at these three sources of information and identify the types of learning you prefer. Activity Sheet 25 can help you to do this.

Although you probably do best in these preferred types of learning, we can use two sources of evidence to test this assumption. The first relies on *your courses*. By analyzing how you do in courses that emphasize different types of learning, you should get some evidence to test this point. For each course you should notice your final grade, the degree of improvement you made during the year, and the types of tests, papers, and projects in which you did well. After this, determine the type(s) of learning required in that course. You should then know which types of learning you can use best.

By looking at your *non-school situations*, you can discover if the same thing is true there. For this, notice the types of tasks which you do well when faced with learning situations at home, in clubs, in church, at camp, and so on. Do these tend to require more rote, association, or problem-solving? For example, how successful are you in solving puzzles as compared to remembering a list of names?

Using both school and non-school information, you should now be able to identify the types of learning you use best. To help you do this, fill in Activity Sheet 26. With this information, you can now see if your preferred types of learning are the same as the ones you use best. Use Activity Sheet 27 for this purpose. This analysis should give you some very valuable information: you will now be able to compare your knowledge about yourself and the types of learning required by your college. Activity Sheet 28 is designed to show this comparison.

If this information shows that your college requires, and that you prefer and can use best, the same types of learning, you have identified another factor that should help you succeed. However, if this is not the case, several other inferences could be drawn.

First, your chances of success are reduced if you do not use best the types of learning required by your college. Second, if you can use, but do not prefer, these types of learning, your success may depend upon changing your preferences. If this is true, you are now faced with the task of changing your existing habits and attitudes. As we mentioned earlier, because of various roadblocks this may not be easy. Perhaps an increased understanding of the types of learning will be beneficial. I have included at the end of this chapter readings by Cronbach, Dudycha, Heyns, and Lindgren who deal with this topic in more depth. If you desire more detailed information about this topic at this time, you can also skip to Chapter XIII where methods of modifying types of learning are discussed more fully.

On the other hand, you may not want to change your preferences. In this instance, you are again faced with the possibility of changing courses, curricula or colleges. This third possibility, of course, may pose more of a problem than the second. Nevertheless, both are important to consider if you are to succeed.

NOTE THESE IDEAS

You have now completed your analysis of the abilities and types of learning required by your college. You have also compared these to the abilities you possess and the types of learning you prefer and can use best. As you made these analyses and comparisons, I have tried to point out their significance for you. As we noted above, where you and your college agree on the required abilities and types of learning, your chances of succeeding are high. Where they do not agree, the opposite is true, and I have pointed out possible courses of action which you may wish to follow.

If you now combine these ideas with your information on goals from Chapter III, you can draw another set of inferences. First, *your greatest chance of obtaining success exists when you and your college are in complete agreement on goals, abilities, and types of learning.* Second, you probably can obtain moderate success if you and your college are in moderate agreement on these factors. Finally, you probably will not succeed if you and your college are very different in terms of these elements.

Before ending this discussion, however, I would like to restate a basic point developed in Chapter I. You and your college are unique. In view of the content of this chapter, this statement should have greater meaning now. Your college's uniqueness includes its particular set of goals, required abilities, and necessary types of learning. Likewise, these factors help to produce your uniqueness. However, since you possess other characteristics (such as habits, attitudes, and personality needs) that also make you unique, it is important that you analyze these also. Further, we shall have to look at additional characteristics of your college. To help you determine with *more precision* your chances for succeeding and what you may have to do to increase your chances, we shall have to see how all of your characteristics function in the most specific unit of your college's uniqueness—the individual course. We shall begin this analysis in the next chapter.

THOUGHT QUESTIONS

1. Name your highest mental, physical, and social abilities. How can you use this information to increase your chances of succeeding in college?
2. Why is it important that you understand which types of learning you prefer and use best? Is it possible to prefer association learning but not use it well? Why?
3. How can your habits, attitudes, or personality needs interfere with your analysis of your abilities? What can you do if this happens?
4. Do you think there is any connection between the reasons why a student attends college and the highest types of abilities he has? Why do you say this?
5. In view of your analysis of your goals, abilities, and types of learning, what are your chances of succeeding in your college? What leads you to draw this conclusion?

SELECTED REFERENCES

Types of Learning

Cronbach, L. J. *Educational Psychology*, rev. ed. New York: Harcourt Brace, 1963. Part C.

Dudycha, George J. *Learn More with Less Effort*. New York: Harper, 1957. Chapters 4–6.

Heyns, Roger W. *The Psychology of Personal Adjustment*. New York: Dryden Press, 1958. Chapter 6.

Lindgren, Henry C. *Psychology of Personal and Social Adjustment*, rev. ed. New York: American, 1959. Chapter 16.

Stephens, J. M. *Educational Psychology*, rev. ed. New York: Holt, 1956. Part 3.

CHAPTER V

Analyzing Course-Demands

In the preceding chapters we have seen that succeeding in college is dependent upon a number of factors. We have also noticed that you will probably succeed if your goals, abilities, and preferred types of learning are similar to those of your college. To increase the level of your success, however, you must meet the specific requirements or course-demands of *each course*. In this chapter I shall explain how you can determine your course-demands.

THE NATURE OF COURSE-DEMANDS

We have already seen that each of your courses has certain goals, requires certain abilities, and emphasizes certain types of learning. In addition to meeting these requirements, you must meet a number of other requirements, both obvious and subtle, if you are to succeed academically. We can say that each course demands certain things from you. *When all of these obvious and subtle requirements are identified, you then can say that you know the course-demands.* If you can meet these, you will achieve academic success in that course. In other words, course-demands represent the uniqueness of a course.

First, I shall discuss some of the obvious types of *course-demands. These are requirements that are clearly observable.* Typically the instructor states them orally in class or they are listed in the syllabus for the course. They include completion of specific *activities* such as reading assignments, oral participation, term papers, oral reports, laboratory experiments, and examinations. It is obvious that you cannot succeed academically if you do not fulfill these requirements. Other obvious course-demands include *regulations* concerning such matters as class attendance, promptness in handing in required work, and common social etiquette.

Although most courses may have these obvious course-demands, you should not assume that all courses do. Likewise, you should not assume that each course's assigned oral reports or term papers require the same preparation. I shall explain this shortly.

Subtle course-demands are requirements that are not easily recognizable. They may or may not be pointed out by the professor, but, in either case, it is not always easy for you to figure out what is required. Subtle course-demands include unstated goals and expectations of the professor, his particular personality traits, pressures from other students, required abilities, and required types of learning. For example, although a teacher may state the goals which he has deliberately set up for a course, he may also have a goal for his students of which *he* is not aware. This unstated goal—let us say conforming to the professor's view of history—is a subtle course-demand because you must meet this requirement if you are to succeed academically in that course.

Another illustration may help you understand subtle course-demands better. If oral participation by the students is encouraged and required by a teacher in one of your courses, the amount and quality of the discussion by the other students acts as a subtle course-demand on you. In this sense, your participation is compared to that of your classmates. If you happen to be with a very verbal group of students, this requirement will be much higher than it would be for a

different group of students. Since you are typically unaware of this comparison, it will be a subtle course-demand for you.

You can see now that our previous discussion in Chapter IV, concerning course goals, required abilities, and required types of learning, really dealt with subtle course-demands. You have already identified some of the course-demands existing in your college; in order to discover others, we need to discuss the methods you can use to determine course-demands. For most courses, these demands include Activities, Regulations, Goals, Types of Abilities, Types of Learning, Teacher Evaluation, Professor's Personality, and Student Pressure.

METHODS OF DETERMINING COURSE-DEMANDS

We have seen that identifying obvious course-demands is not difficult, since they are typically stated in the College Bulletin or the course description distributed by the instructor or presented by the instructor in class. From these sources you should be able to determine class attendance regulations, what written assignments you must hand in, what readings you must study, and the general subject content of the course. Identifying subtle course-demands requires additional methods. These revolve mainly round *careful observation of cues from two sources, the professor and other students.*

The Professor as a Source of Course-Demands

Each teacher, by the way he lectures, leads discussions, conducts laboratories, makes assignments, asks questions, and responds to student inquiries, communicates his course-demands. These cues point to his goals, the kinds of abilities and types of learning he requires, the most important parts of the course content, and the way he will evaluate written assignments and examinations. This is only natural since the course he teaches is, to a large extent, a product of his thinking and personality. This accounts for the uniqueness of each course! It also explains why you cannot assume that another course with a similar title, but taught by a different instructor, will have the same course-demands as the course you are taking.

You can probably understand this better if I discuss the relationship of the professor's activities to the various types of course-demands. There are several ways to determine the professor's *goals*. In addition to his direct written or oral statements on the course's goals, several aspects of his lectures can suggest goals. If he organizes his material and spends a great deal of time on details, this generally means that you must recall this information thoroughly. On the other hand, if he spends most of his time showing relationships among the different aspects of the subject, you will probably have to be able to integrate your knowledge.

Cues regarding goals can also be gleaned from the way the teacher leads discussions and conducts laboratories. If he promotes and encourages individuality in these situations, you can expect him to want his students to be individualistic; however, if he requires you to adhere to a set way of thinking or of carrying out experiments, this would suggest that he expects conformity.

The kinds of assignments given by the professor also suggest goals. When he assigns readings without giving you any specific projects to do or problems to solve, this typically means that he is not concerned with problem-solving as a goal. In contrast, when projects or problems are included, this implies that he wants the student to achieve problem-solving goals in relation to the course's content.

The professor also suggests his goals by the way he asks questions in class and responds to student questions. If he does not ask questions (assuming the class is relatively small), he is probably concerned with covering a certain amount of content but not too worried about the student's comprehension of the content. This, in turn, suggests recall

goals rather than comprehension goals. When he encourages questions, this suggests that he is concerned with comprehension beyond mere recall.

We can also infer goals from the way the professor assigns papers and constructs examinations. The assigned papers may require careful analysis of the literature on a topic, a routine gathering of facts, or creative imagination supported by some factual material. Each type of paper implies different goals. The same can be said of the types of questions the professor uses in his exams. If his questions can be answered by recalling or recognizing simple ideas or facts, he probably has this as a goal, but if he is more concerned with synthesis or creativity, his exams will reflect it. His questions will demand that you express original ideas, supported by material presented in the course. If he thinks you should learn to solve problems, his exams will require that you do this.

You can obtain a good idea of other types of subtle course-demands in the same manner. Analyzing the teacher's activities can suggest the types of abilities and learnings which he requires, the way he will evaluate your work, and any particular demands that are related to his own personality. Without going into too much detail, let me discuss each of these course-demands with several illustrations.

As a result of the discussion in Chapter IV, you know that there are various kinds of abilities and that different courses may require different abilities. Observing the professor's activities can lead to a better understanding of the particular *types of abilities* he requires in his course. For example, the types of assignments, papers, and examinations that he gives can indicate whether he stresses abstract reasoning, physical coordination, simple recall, or critical thinking.

The same activities can also indicate the *types of learning* required in his course. If the exam questions require only that you remember factual material, this suggests that you must emphasize rote and association learning. However, if they demand integration of ideas or figuring out solutions to problems, then rote, association, conscious problem-solving, and unconscious insight are all required.

Another subtle course-demand that is quite different from goals, abilities, or types of learning but is crucial to academic achievement is *teacher evaluation.* Each professor has his own way of judging the worth of the student's work. He may do this by averaging the grades for specific tasks such as papers, exams, oral reports, and laboratory exercises; on the other hand, he may make an overall evaluation, primarily on subjective observation. Some teachers assign grades according to some standard that they believe students should meet; some professors evaluate a student by comparing his work to the work of other students in the same class. Since instructors vary in their evaluation procedures, you must learn what each instructor demands; unfortunately, you can typically obtain these cues only after you have completed the first paper or exam. Nevertheless, you can use this information during the rest of the course.

There is one more subtle course-demand that can be determined by observing the professor's activities. This is the effect of the *professor's personality.* The professor's particular set of personality characteristics may lead him to establish some requirements for his students. Here I am not referring to goals or abilities that are somewhat influenced by his personality; rather, I'm referring to those requirements that are a direct result of his personality. For example, a professor may be very concerned about the neatness of his students' work, so concerned, in fact, that he will evaluate only extremely neat papers and exams. This personality characteristic (course-demand) must be met by his students. Likewise, another instructor may require strict conformity in his students. Or, another professor may require "learning for learning's sake" and look down on vocationally oriented students. Regardless of the type of person-

ality characteristic, if it poses a requirement that you must meet in order to achieve academic success, it is a course-demand.

Students as a Source of Course-Demands

A complete picture of course-demands must also include an observation of the other students. This source of information can supplement observations of the professor, and, in addition, it can give you a different perspective on course requirements. Two types of student observations can be used. The first concerns *observations of other students in the same class.* I have already pointed out that the amount and quality of student discussion can act as a course-demand. In addition, classmates can also create other subtle course-demands. For example, you may find yourself in a class of "brains." Being with especially bright students means that you will have to do better work than if you were in another class. Similarly, your classmates may have a better background for the subject, and this creates another course-demand for you.

You can also use *observations made by students who have already had the course from the same professor.* By talking with several of these students, you can see how they have viewed the instructor and his lectures, assigned readings, papers, and exams, and you can use their observations to obtain a preliminary estimate of the course-demands. After you have started the course, you can check this original estimate. For example, other students may indicate that the instructor requires a great deal of rote memorization. By making your own observations of the professor, you can check their evaluation against your own.

DISCOVERING YOUR COURSE-DEMANDS

We are now ready to determine the course-demands of your courses. Since the aim of this chapter is to help you analyze the smallest unit of your college's uniqueness, we shall figure out the course-demands for *one* of your courses. Following the same procedures, you should be able to establish the course-demands for your other courses later.

Because you have earlier determined the goals, types of abilities, and types of learning required in one course (Chapters III and IV), you already have some data that will be useful. Now we need to incorporate new information about these three kinds of course-demands, as well as attempt to identify other course-demands that exist for you. To help you to do this, I have developed an example of this procedure. I have taken the information concerning Psychology 20 that we discussed in Chapters III and IV and added other data that make it possible to figure out the course-demands for that course. All of this information has been listed in Figure 12.

For a full understanding of this material, follow these ideas carefully. The various kinds of obvious and subtle course-demands have been identified and listed vertically. The seven sources of information have been listed horizontally. As I began the process of identifying Activities, I first checked the college catalogue. Whenever I discovered any information about the Activities required in this course, I listed it in section 1A. Carrying out the same procedure for each source of information, I filled in sections 2A through 5A. Sections 6A and 7A are blank because there is no information about Activities in the listings from Chapters III and IV, since these listings dealt only with Goals, Types of Abilities, and Types of Learning. I then followed the same procedure for each of the other course-demands. Figure 12 incorporates the results of this process.

Several points should be observed about this listing of information. First, even though several sources supply the same data, the data have been listed in each of the appropriate sections. These duplications will be valuable later, when a composite statement of the course-demands is developed. Second, the several sources of data do not always supply the same information. For example, the Oral Course Description of Types of Abilities (3D) is somewhat different from the Observations of Students on Types of Abilities (5D). These kinds of differences are also valuable for developing the composite statement. Third, there is more information about certain course-demands than about others. Compare the detailed information for Regulations (1B–5B) and the scant data for Professor's Personality (1G–5G).

The next step is to determine a composite statement of the course-demands. This is necessary since some overlapping and repetition results from an analysis of the various sources of information (compare 1A and 5A). Each composite statement has been determined by eliminating the duplications and combining the remaining information. Where duplications have existed, the degree of emphasis has been determined and shown by a code system. The composite statement of the course-demands for Psychology 20 appears as Figure 13. Using this information, we can assume that, unless you complete the stated activities, fulfill the regulations, have about the same goals, have a high level of the required abilities, use the same types of learning, and take into account the professor's methods of evaluation and his personality as well as student competition, you will not succeed academically in Psychology 20.

Note something else about Figure 13. It describes everything about this course *except the content*. For complete academic success, you must meet the course-demands established by the content of the course—psychology. You must remember psychological facts! For another course with the same course-demands but a different content (say, history or biology), achieving academic success may prove more difficult because of the different content.

We are now ready for you to make an analysis of one of your own courses. As you begin, keep in mind our earlier discussion regarding roadblocks. Are any of your habits, attitudes, personality needs, or unconscious factors going to interfere with your efforts? If you encounter any difficulties, you might go back to Chapter II and think about these

Figure 12 • COURSE-DEMANDS FOR PSYCHOLOGY 20

Course-Demand	College Bulletin (1)	Printed Course Description (2)	Oral Course Description (3)	Source of Information — Observations of Professor (4)	Observations of Students (5)	Listings of Goals from Chapter III (6)	Listings of Abilities and Learnings from Chapter IV (7)
Activities (A)	read basic text attend field trips	read basic text read extra references attend field trips take midterm and final exams		read basic text attend field trips take midterm and final exams	read basic text take midterm and final exams don't ask questions in class take detailed notes in class		
Regulations (B)	attend class regularly act as a mature student	student permitted 3 class cuts attend all field trips take exams on day given	attendance required except for good reason only 3 class cuts permitted no make-up given except for illness no talking permitted in class sit in assigned seats	attend class except for illness take exams on scheduled day do not disturb professor in class see professor only when don't understand test or lectures			
Goals (C)	to give student survey of whole field of psychology to have student know basic facts related to behavior to help student appreciate importance of psychology in our lives	no information about goals	to get student to remember established psychological facts to have student use scientific method in studying human behavior to have student understand ways that psychology can be used in different occupations	to have student accept facts without questioning them to have student remember facts to cover a certain amount of content to get student interested in field of psychology	to have student memorize detailed facts from textbook to have student answer questions in way professor wants	to give student survey of whole field of psychology to have student understand how psychology is important in lives and occupations to have student use scientific method in studying human beings	
Types of Abilities (D)	*Mental:* reading remembering facts appreciating application of psychology	*Mental:* reading remembering facts	*Mental:* reading remembering facts applying scientific method understanding applications	*Mental:* reading remembering facts developing interest	*Mental:* reading remembering facts figuring out what professor wants	*Mental:* reading remembering facts understanding applications applying scientific method	

Figure 12—Continued

	Source of Information						
Course-Demand	College Bulletin (1)	Printed Course Description (2)	Oral Course Description (3)	Observations of Professor (4)	Observations of Students (5)	Listings of Goals from Chapter III (6)	Listings of Abilities and Learnings from Chapter IV (7)
Types of Learning (E)	rote association	rote association	rote association conscious problem-solving unconscious insight	rote association	rote association	rote association conscious problem-solving unconscious insight	mostly rote association some conscious problem-solving and unconscious insight
Teacher Evaluation (F)			all activities (exams, field trips, class attendance) used for grading	use of "curve" for deriving grades multiple-choice questions on exams average of exam grades	answer all questions guess when don't know answer exam scores and class attendance used for grading		
Professor's Personality (G)				accept professor as authority conform to regulations do not bother professor with details	do not question professor's point of view do not seek help from professor		
Student Pressure (H)	course open to all students	no course prerequisite necessary			upper-class students make stiff competition biology students have good background large classes prevent class discussions		

Figure 13 • COMPOSITE STATEMENT OF COURSE-DEMANDS FOR PSYCHOLOGY 20

Course-Demand	Statement*
Activities (A)	read basic text (1) attend field trips (1) take midterm and final exams (1) read extra references (3) don't ask questions in class (3) take detailed notes in class (3)
Regulations (B)	attend class regularly (1) take only three cuts (1) take exams on scheduled day (1) do not disturb professor (1) act as mature student (3) do not talk in class (3) sit in assigned seat (3) see professor only when don't understand material (3)
Goals (C)	to have student remember psychological facts (1) to give student survey of field (cover content) (1) to have student understand applications of psychology (1) to have student use scientific method (3) to have student accept facts as presented (3) to get student interested in field of psychology (3) to have student answer questions in way professor wants (3)
Types of Abilities (D)	*Mental:* reading (1) remembering facts (1) applying scientific method (2) appreciating applications of psychology (3) developing interest in psychology (3) figuring out what professor wants (3)
Types of Learning (E)	rote (1) association (1) conscious problem-solving (2) unconscious insight (2)
Teacher Evaluation (F)	exam scores (1) attendance (1) answer all questions (3) use of "curve" (3) multiple-choice questions (3) deductions for more than three cuts (3) guess when don't know (3)
Professor's Personality (G)	accept professor as authority without questioning (2) conform to regulations (3) do not bother professor with details (3) do not seek help from professor (3)
Student Pressure (H)	course open to all (3) no prerequisites (3) upper-class students make stiff competition (3) biology students have good background (3) large classes prevent class discussion (3)

* Key for degree of emphasis:
   (1) Considerable duplication in sources
   (2) Some duplication in sources
   (3) No duplication in sources

aspects again. Use Activity Sheets 29 and 30 to determine the course-demands of one of your courses.

After completing this analysis, you will need to carry out the same procedures for your other courses. Once you have done this, you will be ready to look at your self-demands. We shall do this in the next chapter. Following that, we shall compare your course-demands with your self-demands.

CHAPTER SUMMARY

We have seen that each course has a unique set of obvious and subtle requirements—these are the course-demands. They include Activities, Regulations, Goals, Types of Abilities, Types of Learning, Teacher Evaluation, Professor's Personality, and Student Pressure. After finding out how to identify these factors, you have attempted to discover the course-demands of one of your own courses.

THOUGHT QUESTIONS

1. What are course-demands? Why is it important to discover them?
2. How can you "use" your professor in order to determine your course-demands? Is this procedure dishonest? Why?
3. Does figuring out course-demands take too much time that could be spent in studying? Why do you say this?
4. Is it harder to determine course-demands for certain kinds of courses? What is the implication of your answer?
5. Did analyzing your course-demands help you? Why do you say this?

CHAPTER VI

Analyzing Self-Demands

YOUR SUCCESS IN COLLEGE WILL BE FACILITATED if, in addition to analyzing your courses more carefully, you study yourself in greater depth. In this chapter I shall present one method of accomplishing this. After determining your self-demands, you should be in a better position to help yourself succeed.

THE NATURE OF SELF-DEMANDS

As we have seen earlier, each person is unique. We have talked about this uniqueness in terms of goals (success desired), habits, attitudes, personality needs, unconscious factors, abilities, and types of learning.

We have seen that some of these characteristics can act as roadblocks in your attempts to succeed. When you can recognize these potential problems, you can use this knowledge to facilitate your achievement.

You can also view your characteristics in another way. Whether they act as roadblocks or not, we can say that they represent requirements that you place upon yourself. *They do act as requirements because, since they are part of you, they require you to behave in certain ways. You can say that they demand that you carry out certain behaviors.* In this sense we can call them *self-demands.* In other words, you have certain characteristics—self-demands—that *represent your uniqueness and also require you to behave in certain ways.* Your self-demands include Reasons and Goals, Types of Abilities, Types of Learning, Habits, Attitudes, Personality Needs, and Unconscious Factors.

When we can get a good estimate of an individual's self-demands, we can pretty well predict how he will behave in a specific situation. If the situation is college, or, more specifically, a college course, and we know the course-demands, we can accurately predict if that person will meet those course-demands. (I shall apply this concept later to Psychology 20.)

You can now understand why knowing your self-demands is so important. Once you have estimated them, you should be able to determine how well you can meet the course-demands you have already identified. You should realize that this process makes it possible to complete the comparison you made concerning yourself and your college in Chapters III and IV. Moreover, knowing your self-demands and the course-demands means that you can carry out the comparison for the smallest unit—the single course—and thus be more accurate. From this, you should be able to figure out which behaviors you will need to change if you are to succeed in that course. Before you can apply this procedure to yourself, however, we must discuss the methods you can use to determine your self-demands.

METHODS OF DETERMINING SELF-DEMANDS

Determining self-demands requires the same general approach that you used in estimating course-demands: careful observation and synthesis of information. Because you have already identified some of your reasons for going to college, your habits, attitudes, abilities, and preferred types of learning, you have been determining some of your self-demands without identifying them as such. Therefore, you need to review the ways in which you have used certain sources of information. In

addition, I shall indicate other ways in which these sources can be used and point out how all of the data can be synthesized to give you a picture of your self-demands.

Several sources of information were frequently used in Chapters II and IV. These included your *self, high school record, nonschool activities, test results, significant others,* and *college personnel.* Let's look at each of these. By *self, I'm referring to what you now know of yourself, past or present, and how you estimate yourself.* Thus, you used your self when you were figuring out your habits and attitudes, and you used this same source to estimate your reasons for going to college and the types of learning you prefer.

Although you have not yet figured out your personality needs or unconscious factors, you might also use your self to help determine these self-demands. This is not easy because, as I have pointed out in Chapter II, personality needs and unconscious factors are extremely difficult for us to understand and observe. However, it is possible, from time to time, to observe yourself and obtain some insight into these self-demands. Let's look at personality needs first. By asking yourself certain questions, you can obtain your own view (self) of this self-demand.

Concerning the biological needs, take as examples:

1. Do I need a great deal of sleep?
2. Do I require considerable food intake?
3. Do I have strong sexual drives?
4. Do I require lengthy recreation periods?
5. Do I require special medical care?

Concerning the psychological-social needs, take as examples:

1. Do I have a strong desire to win or succeed?
2. Do I require considerable attention and loving from others?
3. Do I have a great desire to help others?

4. Do I require considerable orderliness in my life?
5. Do I greatly desire to be with other people?

Although you may not obtain any comprehensive picture of your personality needs from questions such as these, using your self in this manner can supplement the knowledge of this self-demand which you obtain from other sources. We shall look at those sources shortly.

Using your self in the same manner may give you insight into the unconscious factors that make up another aspect of your self-demands. In this case, however, you will need to ask questions about unusual experiences instead of everyday events. These experiences may deal with your worries, your lapses of memory, or your resistances to certain situations. As examples:

1. Why am I suddenly worried about passing this course?
2. Why did I forget the name of that teacher?
3. Why did I "go blank" on that test?
4. Why do I suddenly feel that I can't stand that course anymore?
5. Why am I putting off studying for that exam?

Although you may not be able to answer these questions accurately, the fact that you have observed your thoughts and feelings about these circumstances means that you are using your self in attempting to understand your unconscious factors. Once again, however, other sources must supplement your efforts to get at this self-demand. We shall discuss these shortly.

It may not appear that your *high school record* will be a very useful source, but you have used it as a source several times earlier. You have used it to determine your highest and lowest mental, physical, and social abilities, the types of learning you prefer, and the types of learning you use best. It may also give you information concerning your personality needs. For example, if you spent a great deal of time and energy in social extra-curricular activities, you may have strong needs to belong and be with others. Likewise, your record may disclose considerable school absences due to illness; this would suggest another aspect of your biological needs. Keep in mind, however, that these two latter illustrations are subject to different interpretations.

Your *non-school activities* have also been helpful in determining your self-demands. You have used this source to estimate your abilities, the types of learning you prefer, and your best types of learning. This source of information can also be used to determine your habits, attitudes, personality needs, and unconscious factors. Let's look at these briefly. Certainly the various activities you carry out in conjunction with your home, social clubs, service organizations, informal peer groups, or religious groups can shed light on these self-demands. For example, the way you fulfill your home tasks can point up your habits at work. The same can be observed of your efforts in social clubs or service organizations.

Similarly, you can gain some insight regarding your attitudes. How you react to your parents, club leaders, or organization leaders should tell you about your attitudes toward authority, while the way you get along with other members of your social clubs and informal peer groups should point out your attitudes toward teenagers.

The same kinds of activities can give you further information about your personality needs. Your reactions may indicate a strong need to dominate others or to gain recognition by others. These same non-school activities may also suggest some unconscious factors: for example, you may observe that you frequently forget to attend your social club meetings, or you might realize that you are frequently disturbed by certain kinds of peers.

You should note that determining self-demands from non-school activities requires considerable subjective interpretation. Using *test results* can check these interpretations, since this source of information tends to be more objective. You have already used this source of information when you were determining your highest and lowest abilities. In addition, you can use test results to get information on the types of learning you can use well, your habits, attitudes, personality needs, and unconscious factors. You will need the aid of a counselor or other test expert to interpret the meanings of the results, but, since most colleges now have these personnel available, it should not prove too difficult to arrange to take such tests and later to discuss the results. You should be able to obtain more information regarding your study habits and attitudes, your ability to perform problem-solving in various fields, and your personality needs.

Another source of information is *significant others*. You can seek out the subjective observations of individuals such as your high school teachers, counselors, principal, group leader, or religious leader, who are called *significant others* because they frequently play extremely important roles in young peoples' lives. They can provide meaningful observations because of their close contact with you, but, at the same time, they can be more objective than your parents.[1] Thus, their observations are very significant for determining self-demands.

You used this source when you were figuring out your highest and lowest abilities. You can also use it to determine your reasons for going to college, your preferred types of learning, habits, attitudes, personality needs, and unconscious factors. Let's discuss this a little. Using significant others can be very beneficial in checking your own

perceptions of why you are attending college. However, your perception may be completely inconsistent with how others see your reasons or goals. Thus, the observations of your high school principal, teachers, and counselors may help you see your reasons more objectively. Likewise, observations by your group leader can point out the types of learning you use best in that situation. Or, further, observations by your religious leader can indicate aspects of your personality needs that show up only in a religious atmosphere.

As I indicated in Chapter IV, you can obtain this information only if you discuss your wishes openly with these people. When you interview them, they must believe that you will interpret their observations accurately and that you will use the information in a constructive way. Otherwise, you will not obtain helpful data.

The same can be said for the next source —*college personnel*. These are the various members of the faculty and staff available to you at your college. They can be your instructors, dormitory advisors, health officers, academic advisors, counselors, financial-aid officers, or deans. If you have had enough contact with any of these people, they can also give you their perceptions of you. In addition, they can interpret any tests which you took during your admissions and orientation process. In this manner, you can use them as a source in determining your self-demands in the same way that you used test results and significant others as sources.

The final source of information is the *college record*, which presents your progress in college. As with the high school record, it should include all facets of your college experience. In particular, it should indicate the areas of academic achievement and participation in extra-curricular activities. Since you probably have not been in college too long, this source may not be as valuable as your high school record. Nevertheless, it should give you some information about your rea-

---

[1] Although parents could also be used as a source of information for determining self-demands, I have not included them because they are generally too subjective. Generally, their perceptions do not add to the student's accurate picture of his self-demands. On the contrary, they may make this picture even less accurate. Certainly the student must consider the influence his parents have had and do have on him, but this influence should be estimated by people other than his parents. *Significant others* can do this.

sons for going to college, your habits, attitudes, abilities, types of learning, personality needs, and unconscious factors.

Several comments can illustrate these possibilities. You should get some insight into your reasons for going to college (goals) by noticing the type of academic program you have taken and the efforts you have made to succeed in it. If you spend much more time in your extra-curricular activities than in your studies, this suggests something about your goals. Likewise, your achievement in various courses (perhaps measured by grades) should indicate your highest abilities. Further, your reactions to various faculty members can point out certain personality needs and unconscious factors. Keep in mind, however, that the interpretations you give to these feelings and behaviors are quite subjective and, thus, should be compared with observations from the other sources.

In the past several pages, we have been discussing the various sources you can use to estimate your self-demands. Now you should be able to see how this information can be integrated into a meaningful picture. We shall apply the same procedures that were used with the data regarding the course-demands of Psychology 20.

To illustrate this, I have taken the data concerning David's habits, attitudes, and abilities (Chapters II and IV, Figures 1, 2, and 5–7), added supplemental information, and filled in Figure 14. This chart represents the first stage in figuring out David's self-demands.

There are several points you should consider in analyzing Figure 14. Notice that the sources of information run horizontally across the chart, while the various self-demands are listed vertically. I have placed the information in the appropriate sections so that it is easy to compare the data from the different sources. Also, notice that I have added considerable data regarding David's goals, preferred types of learning, personality needs, and unconscious factors, since this information was not presented in Chapters II or IV.

After reading the chart, you should realize that the various sources of information provide different amounts of data regarding the self-demands. To illustrate, the high school record contains lots of specific information about David's abilities, but nothing concerning the other self-demands. In contrast, his non-school activities give data for abilities, types of learning, habits, attitudes, and personality needs.

As you study this chart, you will also realize that David's perception of himself does not always agree with how others see him. For example, although he seems to know clearly why he is going to college (1A), others believe he does not have a broad understanding of the goals of college (5A). A difference in perception also exists regarding his attitudes. While David tends to view his submissiveness positively (1E), others see this attitude as a negative characteristic (5E and 6E). On the other hand, the sources of information do agree on a number of points. There is considerable concurrence, for example, on his strongest abilities (2B–7B), and on his helpful mental habits (1D–6D).

In view of these kinds of comparisons, it is possible to synthesize a composite picture of David's self-demands by taking the statements that are identical or very similar and listing them. They are then coded, according to the amount of duplication. In this way it is possible to identify David's most important self-demands. Figure 15 presents this information.

From these data, it appears that David is attending college primarily because of his parents' wishes. Further, it seems that he will probably do best in remembering specific facts and information, but that he will do poorly in problem-solving or creative work. He is likely to do well in courses that require detailed memorization, are highly organized, do not demand creative thinking, are not too

Figure 14 • DAVID'S SELF-DEMANDS

Self-Demands (A)	Self (1)	High School Record (2)	Non-School Activities (3)	Test Results (4)	Significant Others (5)	College Personnel (6)	College Record (7)
Reasons and Goals (A)	want to become an accountant; want to learn more about society; want to get along with people better; all my friends are going to college; parents want me to go to college				determined to get a college degree; parents want him to go to college; interested in numbers but not mathematics; lacks any broad understanding of goals of college		highly specialized curriculum; no extra-curricular activities
Types of Abilities (B) — Highest		*Mental* remembering facts; answering specific questions; looking up information; answering questions in class *Physical* running on track team *Social* getting along with a few friends; taking part in student council; taking part in class committee meetings	*Mental* passed Boy Scout merit tests; remembered church regulations; passed driver's written test *Physical* passed Boy Scout hike tests *Social* having friends at home; got along well with Boy Scouts; get along well with adults	*Mental* numerical; language; clerical; social studies; language usage	*Mental* best at specific things	*Mental* remembering factual data; using numbers; spelling	*Mental* did well in accounting course
Types of Abilities (B) — Lowest		*Mental* solving mathematical problems; creating poetry; using chemical equations *Physical* playing team sports; achieving coordination in shop courses; completing physical fitness tests	*Mental* can't solve crossword puzzles; get beaten in chess or checkers *Physical* avoid contact sports; not handy with tools at home	*Mental* spatial relations; mechanical; abstract; mathematics	*Physical* physical stamina and ability	*Mental* critical thinking; abstract thinking; analytical reading; essay writing *Physical* coordination; stamina	*Mental* did poorly in English course; did poorly in philosophy course *Physical* did poorly in physical education tests

Source of Information

Figure 14—Continued

Self-Demands	Source of Information						
	Self (1)	High School Record (2)	Non-School Activities (3)	Test Results (4)	Significant Others (5)	College Personnel (6)	College Record (7)
		Social making new friends joining a fraternity	*Social* have a hard time getting dates have a hard time making new friends did poorly in part-time selling job		*Social* meeting and socializing with new people		
Types of Learning (C)	*Prefer:* rely on rote in studying like courses with clearcut division between right and wrong information *Do Best:* memorize while studying		*Prefer:* like to have others indicate the correct way of doing things *Do Best:* memorized regulations in Scouts and church		*Prefer:* avoids trying to solve new problems likes order in what has to be learned *Do Best:* remembers facts by rote	*Prefer:* likes clearcut factual material *Do Best:* recalls simple facts	*Do Best:* remembering specific facts
Habits (D) — Which Help	*Mental* check work carefully very precise in work always complete tasks on time *Social* polite to others listen to older people *Physical* keep self clean do not smoke		*Mental* perform home tasks carefully completed Scout tasks on time carry out church responsibilities *Social* followed directions of Scout leaders abide by social groups' decisions		*Mental* always completes tasks works very neatly *Social* always polite *Physical* dresses neatly well groomed eats healthy food	*Mental* hands work in on time	
Habits (D) — Which Hinder	*Mental* read slowly lose concentration easily		*Mental* daydream a lot at home		*Mental* reads without precision can't concentrate for long relies on others for ideas	*Mental* gives up easily on hard assignments	

Figure 14—Continued

Source of Information

Self-Demands	Self (1)	High School Record (2)	Non-School Activities (3)	Test Results (4)	Significant Others (5)	College Personnel (6)	College Record (7)
	Social rarely join groups		*Social* didn't take leadership role in scouts		*Social* never tries to lead groups follows groups in anything		
	Physical get tired easily		*Physical* can't stay out late without getting tired		*Physical* nervous habits with hands		
Attitudes (E)	*Positive* like most teachers enjoy school most of time don't mind hard work willing to follow good leaders		*Positive* like Scout and group leaders enjoy other teenagers strong belief in religious teachings		*Positive* willing to work hard tries to please others routinely enjoys school	*Positive* willing to listen to suggestions	
	Negative dislike "talky" teachers dislike non-practical school subjects don't like rough sports		*Negative* don't like "forward" teenagers not willing to push self to get dates		*Negative* too willing to let others dominate	*Negative* responds passively to criticism	
Personality Needs (F)	*Biological* require lots of sleep				*Biological* fatigues easily requires lots of food		
	Psychological want to succeed very much want people to like me		*Psychological* want to conform to leader's wishes want to be with others		*Psychological* high achievement drive desires order in work	*Psychological* like everything orderly	*Psychological* prefer clear and orderly subject matter
Unconscious Factors (G)	went "blank" on English final exam put off writing philosophy term paper				not clear as to influence of parents unaware of nervous habits		

Figure 15 • COMPOSITE STATEMENT OF DAVID'S SELF-DEMANDS

Self-Demand	Statement*
Reasons and Goals (A)	parents want me to go to college (2) all my friends are going to college (3) want to become an accountant (3) want to learn more about society (3) want to learn to get along with people better (3) determined to get a college degree (3) interested in numbers but not mathematics (3) lacks any broad understanding of goals of college (3) taking highly specialized curriculum (3) doesn't participate in extra-curricular activities (3)
Types of Abilities (B) — Highest	*Mental* remembering specific facts and information (1) using numbers (2) answering specific questions (2) looking up information (3) language (3) clerical (3) social studies (3) language usage (3) spelling (3) *Physical* running on track team (3) passed Boy Scout hike tests (3) *Social* getting along with close peers (2) taking part in organized school groups (2) getting along with adults (3)
Types of Abilities (B) — Lowest	*Mental* doing problem-solving in all situations (1) doing abstract thinking (1) creating poetry (3) critical thinking (3) analytical reading (3) essay-writing (3) spatial relations (3) mechanical (3) mathematics (3) *Physical* coordination (1) physical stamina (2) playing contact sports (2) completing physical fitness tests (2) *Social* meeting and making friends (1) joining a fraternity (3) getting dates (3) did poorly in part-time selling job (3)
Types of Learning (C)	*Prefer:* likes order and clearcut material (1) relies on rote in studying (3) likes others to indicate correct way of doing things (3) avoids trying to solve new problems (3) *Do Best:* memorizing by rote specific information (1) recalling simple facts (2)

Figure 15—Continued

Self-Demand	Statement*
Habits (D) — Which Help	*Mental* does work carefully (1) hands work in on time (1) work is neat and precise (2) *Social* polite to others (2) listens to older people (2) abides by social groups' decisions (3) *Physical* keeps self clean and neat (2) does not smoke (3) eats healthy food (3)
Habits (D) — Which Hinder	*Mental* can't concentrate for long (1) reads slowly and without precision (2) relies on others for ideas (3) gives up easily on hard assignments (3) *Social* doesn't take leadership role (2) rarely joins groups (3) follows groups in anything (3) *Physical* gets tired easily (2) has nervous habits with hands (3)
Attitudes (E)	*Positive* tries to please and follow others (2) is willing to work hard (2) enjoys school (2) likes most authority figures (2) enjoys other teenagers (3) has strong belief in religious teachings (3) *Negative* too willing to be submissive to others (1) dislikes "talky" teachers (3) dislikes non-practical subjects (3) doesn't like rough sports (3)
Personality Needs (F)	*Biological* requires lot of sleep because of fatigue (3) requires lot of food (3) *Psychological* likes order in everything (1) wants to succeed to a great extent (2) submits to others' wishes (2) wants others to like him (3) wants to be with people (3)
Unconscious Factors (G)	went "blank" on English final exam (3) put off writing philosophy term paper (3) not clear as to influence of parents (3) unaware of nervous habits (3)

* Key for degree of emphasis:
    (1) Considerable duplication in source
    (2) Some duplication in sources
    (3) No duplication in sources

abstract and do not involve large amounts of difficult reading. We shall see the implications of this information when we compare David's self-demands with the course-demands of Psychology 20.

DETERMINING YOUR SELF-DEMANDS

You should now be ready to determine your self-demands. You can do this by following the procedures described above. Use the information from Chapters II–IV, where you identified your reasons for going to college, your habits, your attitudes, your highest and lowest abilities, and the types of learning you prefer and use best. If you feel you do not understand the nature of self-demands in enough detail at this time, you can skip ahead to Chapters VIII–XIII where various aspects of each self-demand are dealt with more thoroughly. Complete Activity Sheets 31 and 32 when you are ready to make this analysis.

We will pause here to see if you are encountering any difficulties in completing this procedure. Are any roadblocks getting in the way? As you now know, some of the self-demands that you are trying to identify (habits, attitudes, personality needs, and un-conscious factors) may actually be road-blocks! In view of our discussion in Chapter II, it should not surprise you if you are having difficulty in identifying these self-demands. If this is true for you, perhaps this is where your advisor or counselor would be especially helpful.

Assuming that you have determined your self-demands, you are now ready to see how they can help or hinder your efforts to meet your course-demands. We shall carry out this analysis in the next chapter.

CHAPTER SUMMARY

We have seen that self-demands are those characteristics that require you to carry out certain behaviors. They represent your uniqueness and can be classified as Reasons and Goals, Types of Abilities, Types of Learning, Habits, Attitudes, Personality Needs, and Unconscious Factors. Various sources of information can be used to determine your self-demands: they include the self, the high school record, non-school activities, test results, significant others, and college personnel. Using this information, you have carried out an analysis of your own self-demands.

THOUGHT QUESTIONS

1. How can determining self-demands help a student succeed in college? Can he succeed without making such an analysis? Why?
2. What difficulties might a student encounter when he tries to analyze his self-demands? Why?
3. Did *you* encounter any difficulties when you were determining your self-demands? Why?
4. What sources of information were most helpful to you when you analyzed your self-demands? Which were least helpful? Why?
5. Which of your identified self-demands seem to have the most significance for your chances of succeeding in college? What implications do they suggest for your studying?

CHAPTER VII

Comparing Course-Demands
with Self-Demands

WE ARE NOW READY TO BRING TOGETHER OUR discussions of course-demands and self-demands and see how they can be compared. Such an analysis should make it possible for you to determine quite accurately your chances of gaining academic success. It should also point out the types of modifications that you must make in order to increase your level of success. In this chapter, I shall first show you how to make this comparison, and we shall then discuss its implications for you.

METHOD OF COMPARING COURSE-DEMANDS WITH SELF-DEMANDS

Assuming that specific sets of course-demands and self-demands have been determined, comparing the two is quite simple. You can do this by analyzing each set and identifying the similarities and differences in the data. This will then show you which self-demands you should be concerned with if you want to increase your chances of succeeding.

I shall illustrate this process by comparing the composite list of course-demands for Psychology 20 (Figure 13) and the composite list of David's self-demands (Figure 15). First I reviewed all of the course-demands. Then I studied the list of Activities and saw that there were six statements of Activities. I then turned to Figure 15 and read carefully the statements for each self-demand. When I found a factor that seemed to fit the listed Activities, I wrote the specific item in the appropriate space in Figure 16 and also listed the source for this item. I did the same thing when I identified data that did not fit the listed statements of Activities. I then proceeded to carry out the same kind of comparison for the other course-demands listed in Figure 13. Thus, I studied the list of Regulations and compared it with the data from Figure 15; then I moved on to Goals, Types of Abilities, Types of Learning, and so on. Figure 16 incorporates the completed comparison.

You should note several things as you study this figure. First, many more statements (specific data) fit the course-demands than do not. In fact, there is only one course-demand—Student Pressure—for which there are more statements that do not fit than do fit. This general observation suggests that David will be academically successful in Psychology 20. We shall look at that point in more detail shortly.

Second, a number of specific data are used for several course-demands. For example, one of David's attitudes, "willing to work hard," (Self-Demand E, from Figure 15) is listed as fitting the course-demands under Activities, Types of Learning, Teacher Evaluation, and Professor's Personality. If we identify those statements that are used frequently, we can easily see which self-demands are crucial in satisfying a particular set of course-demands. After carefully analyzing Figure 16 (1), I was able to identify fourteen statements that were listed for at least four different course-demands. These are included in Figure 17. It is interesting to note that most of these statements refer to three of David's self-demands (C, E, and F). In other words, David meets the course-demands of Psychology 20 primarily by the way he learns, his attitudes, and his personality needs.

A third observation you should make about Figure 16 is that all the sources of information provide data about David's self-demands with the exception of Unconscious Factors. Although several statements are listed for this self-demand, Figure 15 (G), these statements do not relate to any of the course-demands and, therefore, are not listed in (1) or (3) in Figure 16. For another course, however, they may be useful.

You should also observe one final point. We can determine from Figure 16 (3) which of David's characteristics must be changed if he is to gain maximum academic success in Psychology 20. Since the specific data listed in (3) do not fit the course-demands, they will not help David succeed in that course. Thus, one of his habits—"can't concentrate for long"—does not fit the course-demands of Activities, Goals, Types of Abilities, Types of Learning, and Student Pressure. I shall return to the factors which do not "fit" below.

We can carry out one last step in our comparison of course-demands and self-demands. Because the prior step has resulted in such a long and detailed chart (Figure 16), it is hard to obtain a brief overall picture of how well an individual's self-demands fit a particular set of course-demands. Some type of summary would make it easier to determine this at a glance, and it would also simplify the process of identifying the course-demands that are most successfully and least successfully met. To develop this summary, we need only to estimate the number of specific data on self-demands that fit and do not fit the course-demands. In this way, we can determine whether the course-demands are met to a great extent, moderately, or slightly. We can also see if the self-demands are actually contrary to the course-demands.

Now let's apply this procedure. I have

Figure 16 • COMPARISON OF DAVID'S SELF-DEMANDS WITH PSYCHOLOGY 20 COURSE-DEMANDS*

Psychology 20 Course-Demand	Self-Demands Which Fit Course-Demands		Self-Demands Which Do Not Fit Course-Demands	
	Specific Data (1)	Source of Information (2)	Specific Data (3)	Source of Information (4)
Activities (A)	likes order and clearcut material	Types of Learning		
	does work carefully	Habits	can't concentrate for long	Habits
			reads slowly and without precision	Habits
	work is neat and precise	Habits		
	listens to older people	Habits		
	willing to work hard	Attitudes		
	likes school	Attitudes		
	likes most authority figures	Attitudes		
	likes order in everything	Personality Needs		
	wants to succeed to a great extent	Personality Needs		
Regulations (B)	likes others to indicate correct way of doing things	Types of Learning		
	polite to others	Habits		
	listens to older people	Habits		
	hands work in on time	Habits		
	tries to please and follow others	Attitudes		
	enjoys school	Attitudes		
	likes most authority figures	Attitudes		
	likes order in everything	Personality Needs		
	submits to others' wishes	Personality Needs		
Goals (C)	determined to get a college degree	Reasons and Goals	parents want him to go to college	Reasons and Goals
	wants to learn more about society	Reasons and Goals	all his friends are going to college	Reasons and Goals
	wants to learn to get along with people better	Reasons and Goals	wants to become an accountant	Reasons and Goals
			lacks any broad understanding of goals of college	Reasons and Goals

Figure 16—Continued

Psychology 20 Course-Demand	Self-Demands Which Fit Course-Demands		Self-Demands Which Do Not Fit Course-Demands	
	Specific Data (1)	Source of Information (2)	Specific Data (3)	Source of Information (4)
	able to remember specific facts and information	Types of Abilities	avoids doing problem-solving in all situations	Types of Abilities
	able to answer specific questions	Types of Abilities		
	likes order and clearcut material	Types of Learning	avoids trying to solve problems	Types of Learning
	relies on rote studying	Types of Learning		
	likes others to indicate the correct way of doing things	Types of Learning		
	memorizes by rote specific information	Types of Learning		
	able to recall simple facts	Types of Learning		
	listens to older people	Habits	can't concentrate for long	Habits
	tries to please and follow others	Attitudes	dislikes non-practical subjects	Attitudes
	enjoys school	Attitudes		
	likes most authority figures	Attitudes		
	wants to succeed to a great extent	Personality Needs		
	submits to others' wishes	Personality Needs		
Types of Abilities (D)	wants to learn more about society	Reasons and Goals	avoids doing problem-solving in all situations	Types of Abilities
	wants to learn to get along with people better	Reasons and Goals	avoids doing abstract thinking	Types of Abilities
	remembers specific facts and information	Types of Abilities	avoids trying to solve new problems	Types of Learning
	likes order and clearcut material	Types of Learning		
	relies on rote in studying	Types of Learning		
	memorizes by rote specific information	Types of Learning		
	able to recall simple facts	Types of Learning		
	does work carefully	Habits	can't concentrate for long reads slowly and without precision	Habits Habits

Figure 16—Continued

Psychology 20 Course-Demand	Self-Demands Which Fit Course-Demands		Self-Demands Which Do Not Fit Course-Demands	
	Specific Data (1)	Source of Information (2)	Specific Data (3)	Source of Information (4)
	tries to please and follow others	Attitudes		
	likes most authority figures	Attitudes		
Types of Learning (E)	remembers specific facts and information	Types of Abilities	avoids doing problem-solving in all situations	Types of Abilities
			avoids doing abstract thinking	Types of Abilities
	likes order and clearcut material	Types of Learning	avoids trying to solve new problems	Types of Learning
	relies on rote in studying	Types of Learning		
	memorizes by rote specific information	Types of Learning		
	able to recall simple facts	Types of Learning		
	does work carefully	Habits	can't concentrate for long	Habits
	willing to work hard	Attitudes		
	likes order in everything	Personality Needs		
Teacher Evaluation (F)	determined to get a college degree	Reasons and Goals		
	remembers specific facts and information	Types of Abilities		
	answers specific questions	Types of Abilities		
	relies on rote in studying	Types of Learning		
	memorizes by rote specific information	Types of Learning		
	recalls simple facts	Types of Learning		
	does work carefully	Habits	reads slowly and without precision	Habits
	tries to please and follow others	Attitudes		
	willing to work hard	Attitudes		
	enjoys school	Attitudes		
	likes most authority figures	Attitudes		
	likes order in everything	Personality Needs		
	wants to succeed to a great extent	Personality Needs		
	submits to others' wishes	Personality Needs		

Figure 16—Continued

Psychology 20 Course-Demand	Self-Demands Which Fit Course-Demands		Self-Demands Which Do Not Fit Course-Demands	
	Specific Data (1)	Source of Information (2)	Specific Data (3)	Source of Information (4)
Professor's Personality (G)	gets along with adults	Types of Abilities		
	likes others to indicate correct way of doing things	Types of Learning		
			gives up easily on hard assignments	Habits
	polite to others	Habits		
	listens to older people	Habits		
	tries to please and follow others	Attitudes		
	willing to work hard	Attitudes		
	likes most authority figures	Attitudes		
	likes order in everything	Personality Needs		
	wants to succeed to a great extent	Personality Needs		
	submits to others' wishes	Personality Needs		
Student Pressure (H)	determined to get college degree	Reasons and Goals		
			can't concentrate for long	Habits
			gives up easily on hard assignments	Habits
			reads slowly and without precision	Habits
	wants to succeed to a great extent	Personality Needs		

* David's information about his self-demands comes from Figure 15. Information about the course-demands of Psychology 20 comes from Figure 13.

Figure 17 • DAVID'S SELF-DEMANDS THAT MOST FREQUENTLY FIT THE COURSE-DEMANDS OF PSYCHOLOGY 20*

Self-Demand	Specific Data
Reasons and Goals (A)	
Types of Abilities (B)	remembers specific facts and information
Types of Learning (C)	likes order and clearcut material relies on rote studying memorizes by rote specific information recalls simple facts
Habits (D)	does work carefully listens to older people
Attitudes (E)	willing to work hard enjoys school likes most authority figures tries to please and follow others
Personality Needs (F)	likes order in everything wants to succeed to a great extent submits to others' wishes
Unconscious Factors (G)	

* Only those data on self-demands that were listed for four or more Psychology 20 course-demands are included in this figure.

compared the amount of data listed for self-demands in the first column of Figure 16 (1) (fit column), with those placed in (3) (non-fit column). If all or almost all of these data for a course-demand are placed in (1), the course-demand has been met to a *great* extent. If most of the data (but not all or almost all) is placed there, the course-demand has been met to a *moderate* extent. If about half the data is placed in (1) and half in (3), the course demand has been met to a *slight* extent. In contrast, if all or almost all of the data is placed in (3), the self-demands are *negative*, since they do *not* meet the specific course-demands.

After analyzing the data in Figure 16 in this way, I have checked the appropriate columns in Figure 18. As you can see, the result is a check sheet that tells us at once that David's self-demands fit the course-demands of Psychology 20 to a great or moderate extent, for all but one of the course-demands. As I indicated above, this points out that David should achieve academic success in this course.

Figure 18 also clearly shows where David needs to change his characteristics and his behavior if he wants to increase his *level* of success. Thus, his self-demands, in relation to the course-demands of Goals, Types of Abilities, Types of Learning, and Student Pressure, need modification. To identify the specific self-demands needing change, he would have to study Figure 16. As I noted above, one of these self-demands is his habit of not being able to concentrate. I have identified all of these specific self-demands and listed them in Figure 19. As you will note, David would probably not be able to modify some of these self-demands (poor in abstract thinking), but he could change others (reads slowly and without precision).

One final point should be made here. Although David's self-demands should help him succeed in Psychology 20, they may not help him in another course. Thus, his English course might require more problem-solving and creative abilities. In this course, David's level of success would be lower unless he were able to modify this self-demand.

Figure 18 • SUMMARY COMPARISON OF DAVID'S SELF-DEMANDS WITH COURSE-DEMANDS OF PSYCHOLOGY 20

Course-Demands of Psychology 20	Extent to Which David's Self-Demands Fit These Course-Demands			
	Great (1)	Moderate (2)	Slight (3)	Negative (4)
Activities (A)	X			
Regulations (B)	X			
Goals (C)		X		
Types of Abilities (D)		X		
Teacher Evaluation (F)	X			
Professor's Personality (G)	X			
Student Pressure (H)			X	

Figure 19 • DAVID'S SELF-DEMANDS THAT DO NOT FIT COURSE-DEMANDS OF PSYCHOLOGY 20

Self-Demand	Specific Data*
Reasons and Goals (A)	parents want me to go to college all my friends are going to college want to become an accountant lacks any broad understanding of goals of college
Types of Abilities (B)	unable to do problem-solving in all situations (1) unable to do abstract thinking (1)
Types of Learning (C)	avoid trying to solve new problems (1)
Habits (D)	can't concentrate for long (2) read slowly and without precision (1) give up easily on hard assignments (1)
Attitudes (E)	dislike non-practical subjects
Personality Needs (F)	
Unconscious Factors (G)	

* Key:
(1) Listed for more than one course-demand
(2) Most frequently listed characteristic

COMPARING YOUR COURSE-DEMANDS WITH YOUR SELF-DEMANDS

This discussion has pointed out that, when you complete the comparison of your course-demands with your self-demands, you should be able to identify the particular characteristics that will aid or hinder your academic success in a specific course. To arrive at that point, you will need to follow the same procedures I carried out for David. This should not be difficult if you complete Activity Sheets 33–36.

Assuming that you have finished comparing your self-demands with the course-demands of one of your subjects, you should pause and see what this information means to you. You should realize, of course, that you have made this comparison for only *one* of your current courses. Therefore, if you want to increase your overall academic achievement, you will need to carry out a similar comparison for your other courses. This procedure should be simpler now, since you have already figured out your self-demands. In most cases, these will remain the same from course to course.

There is another way of viewing this information. Because you have identified certain self-demands that do not fit your course-demands, you are now faced with the task of deciding what to do about this situation. You can decide to change some of your self-demands. Or, possibly, you may decide to keep yourself as you are but change your courses, your curriculum, or your college. Further, you can decide that academic success is not really very important to you and, thus, ignore this information and concentrate your energies on achieving another type of success. (We have already discussed these other types in Chapter III.)

The decision you make at this point is very crucial. If you decide to seek non-academic success, you should be aware of the various outcomes of such an action. You may want to talk to your advisor or counselor about your decision before plunging ahead. If you decide to change courses, curricula, or colleges, a discussion with these college personnel will also prove valuable. If, however, you decide to modify some of your self-demands, you should find the next section of this book extremely valuable. When you have finished it, you should have greater knowledge of yourself and some practice in changing yourself to fit the course-demands of your college.

THOUGHT QUESTIONS

1. Was it difficult for you to compare your course-demands with your self-demands? Why?
2. Which of your self-demands best meet your course-demands? Were you aware of this before you made this comparison? Why?
3. To what extent do your self-demands meet your course-demands? What are the implications of your answer?
4. Which self-demands least successfully meet your course-demands? Were you surprised by this information? Why?
5. In view of your comparison, what do you need to do to increase your level of academic success? Do you think you can do this? Why?

SELECTED REFERENCES

On Analyzing Your College

Bennett, Margaret E. *Getting the Most Out of College*. New York: McGraw-Hill, 1957, Chapter 2.

Coleman, James C., and others. *Success in College*. Chicago: Scott Foresman, 1960. Chapter 2.

Morgan, Clifford T., and Deese, James. *How to Study*. New York: McGraw-Hill, 1957. Chapter 1.

On Self-Analysis

Garrison, Roger H. *The Adventure of Learning in College*. New York: Harper, 1959. Chapters 2, 7.

Heyns, Roger W. *The Psychology of Personal Adjustment*. New York: Dryden Press, 1958. Chapter 6.

Lindgren, Henry C. *Psychology of Personal and Social Adjustment*, rev. ed. New York: American, 1959. Chapters 2, 4.

Rogers, Dorothy. *The Psychology of Adolescence*. New York: Appleton-Century-Crofts, 1962. Part 2.

Strang, Ruth. *The Adolescent Views Himself*. New York: McGraw-Hill, 1957. Chapters 1, 3.

SECTION TWO

Modifying Your Self-Demands

CHAPTER VIII

Unconscious Factors, Personality Needs, and Attitudes

In view of our discussion in Chapter VII, you now realize that the achievement of academic success depends upon how well your self-demands fit the course-demands of your college. However, we also know that, for most students, meeting the course-demands will require modification of some self-demands. At this point, then, we need to look at the various ways that self-demands can be modified.

In this and the next five chapters, I shall indicate the difficulties in changing each major type of self-demand, point out the alternatives available, and spell out the procedures that can be used to modify it. In Chap-

ter XIV, I will show how you can apply these ideas to yourself. With this background, you should be in a better position to modify your behavior in order to obtain the success you desire.

DIFFICULTIES IN MODIFYING SELF-DEMANDS

It would be very nice if we could easily modify our self-demands. The truth is, however, that to change most of them requires considerable effort, at least partly because they represent significant characteristics that cannot be shed quickly. Further, most have evolved over a long period of time, and the process has typically occurred in social situations, such as the home and school, that have had emotional overtones. These emotional conditions mean that almost all self-demands have some emotional aspects, which complicate their modification. Changing highly emotional self-demands is much more difficult than changing mildly tinged ones.

If a self-demand is based primarily on emotion, your conscious thinking processes will not have much impact on it. Rather, change will come about only when you feel emotionally secure. Thus, changing this type of self-demand is very dependent on the attitudes and behavior of other people toward you and on your experiences while attempting to change. Only if you are secure in a certain situation will you feel free enough to attempt to change this kind of self-demand, since it has typically evolved through emotionally charged situations such as the family.

Thus, if you desire to change an attitude (an emotionally based self-demand), it is unlikely that you can simply say "I don't like it" and proceed to have a different attitude. Nor is it likely to disappear when you rationally figure out how you obtained this attitude. Its modification is much more dependent upon the experiences you have while attempting to change it. If people accept your behavior and are not hostile toward you while you are attempting to change, you will feel secure and your emotions will not cause you to become defensive. Likewise, if you gain other satisfactions in this process, change becomes more likely.

As an illustration, let's look at our friend David. We saw that one of David's attitudes did not fit his course-demands. His negative feeling for non-practical subjects was inconsistent with the demands of Psychology 20. If David wants to change this attitude, he cannot do so simply by saying to himself: "I will like non-practical subjects; I will like non-practical subjects." Trying to convince himself in this manner will only frustrate him further. In addition to wanting to change, David will have to experience satis-

faction while attempting to do so. Perhaps his friends, teachers, and parents can support him in his efforts. Likewise, if he is successful in a non-practical course, this positive feeling will help him to change his attitude.

In contrast, when a self-demand does not involve a great deal of emotion, change is much more dependent upon the conscious thinking processes. Through logical reasoning, the cause of the difficulty can be determined and necessary remedial steps planned. Assuming that you have inherited the needed intellectual potential, change is then dependent upon your willingness to practice the new behavior. Thus, David's poor reading ability can be modified by the above process, assuming, of course, that other aspects of his self-demands (such as personality needs) do not interfere with this procedure.

This discussion suggests that we cannot separate completely the self-demands that are emotionally charged from those that are not. Even if a self-demand is largely free of emotional involvement (such as a mental ability), attempts to change it may bring into play other self-demands. If these latter are heavily charged emotionally (especially unconscious factors), then changing the former becomes harder.

I must mention another element that makes changing self-demands difficult. As I have pointed out earlier, you will not always be aware of these characteristics. In Chapter II I explained why you may not be aware of your habits and attitudes, are frequently unaware of your personality needs, and are rarely aware of your unconscious factors. It is obvious that, when you are unaware of such characteristics, you cannot make a conscious effort to change them. As a result, they tend to remain the same. The more a self-demand is unknown to you, the more difficult it is to modify it.

Using these ideas, we can list the self-demands in descending order, from most difficult to change to least difficult to change, in this way: unconscious factors, personality needs, attitudes, habits, reasons and goals, types of abilities, and types of learning.

This continuum indicates the different degrees of change possible, in general, for each self-demand. There are three exceptions, however, that you should note. First, although types of learning as a self-demand are listed as very open to modification, this holds true for only three types of learning: trial and error, rote, and association. It is not so for conscious problem-solving and unconscious insight. Because genetic factors, emotions, and the unconscious are involved with the latter two types, modifying them is more difficult. I shall discuss this point in more detail later.

Second, because there are so many different kinds of abilities, listing this self-demand as easily modifiable is not entirely accurate: those higher mental abilities and physical abilities that are primarily dependent upon heredity and those social abilities dependent upon emotional relationships are not easy to change. Many other abilities are quite modifiable, however. Again, I shall discuss the exceptions in more detail later.

The third and final exception concerns habits as self-demands. Most of these are reasonably subject to change, except certain mental and physical habits that are very influenced by personality needs and unconscious factors. We shall look at this point later also.

To help you better understand the ways that self-demands can be modified, I have taken the above listing and separated those that are most difficult from those that are least difficult to change. In this chapter I shall deal with the former, starting with unconscious factors; I shall discuss the difficulties involved in changing and the alternatives available for changing, explain them in more detail, and point out the ways in which changes can be achieved. I shall do the same for the more modifiable self-demands in the following chapters.

UNCONSCIOUS FACTORS

You remember from Chapter II that it is very difficult to become aware of unconscious factors. By definition they are not a part of your awareness; in addition, they are very frequently of an emotional nature. Because of these conditions, it is extremely difficult to modify consciously this self-demand. The major exception to this rule concerns those habits or other behaviors that others can easily observe, although you are not aware of them. However, the rule holds for both thoughts or feelings that are in the unconscious part of the personality and for those unconscious processes which you use in dealing with problems.

Because of the great difficulty in modifying this self-demand, there are very few courses open when you want to change it. One possibility, however, is to ignore it. (Most of us select this alternative without realizing it.) In this case you would carry on your efforts to succeed without paying any attention to this part of yourself. If someone points out a characteristic that you are not aware of, you will typically try to avoid dealing with it. (Incidentally, this process is probably unconscious too!) Proceeding in this manner, however, means that you will be unable to modify this self-demand.

Another alternative available is to try to be alert to the presence of unconscious factors. As I mentioned in Chapter VI, certain unusual behaviors may give you cues that your unconscious is functioning. By noting these situations you may become aware of how this self-demand is interfering with your efforts to succeed. For example, if you "blacked out" in an exam, even though you had previously learned the information very carefully and could recall it before starting the exam, this would suggest that some aspect of your unconscious was controlling your behavior.

Although you may not be able to understand this behavior, its observation leads to another alternative: you can turn to others to help you understand this self-demand. With the help of your advisor or counselor, or the psychologist or psychiatrist at your college, you may be able to gain more knowledge of the way the unconscious works and probably some insights into its significance in your efforts to succeed.

In order for you to utilize the latter two alternatives, I shall now discuss in more detail the various kinds of unconscious factors that make up this self-demand, how they are related to course-demands, and some possible ways to modify them. Because personality needs are listed as a separate self-demand, even though they represent one major part of the unconscious, they will not be discussed in this section. The other unconscious factors will be placed in two major groups: those which are *frustration-related* and those which are *gratification-related.*[1]

Frustration-Related Unconscious Factors

Frustration-related unconscious factors refer to those feelings and processes that result when your personality needs are threatened or are not satisfied. If either of these conditions exists, we can say that you are in a *state of frustration.* If you are unaware of this condition, it is then an unconscious factor affecting your behavior. Usually several other factors are associated with this state. *Anxiety exists when you feel your need satisfaction is being threatened.* Instead of understanding this situation, you only sense that something is wrong but are unable to identify it. You feel tense (anxious) but are unable to explain why. Because of this condition, you tend to feel inadequate and carry out disorganized behavior that does not help you reach your goals or satisfy your needs.

On the other hand, you may sometimes react to this state of frustration in more intense ways. Your *fear* may become so strong that you become rigid and immobile. Or perhaps your *anger* and *hostility* are expressed openly and violently. Sometimes, however, they are expressed subtly and indirectly.

Regardless of the way in which you express these emotions, much of the time you

do so without realizing what you are doing; you are, therefore, motivated by unconscious factors. In addition to these emotional reactions, you also carry on some unconscious defensive processes. You learn to use a whole series of *defense mechanisms* to handle this frustration. They generally take one of three forms: substitution, deception, or withdrawal. If you use *substitution, you will unconsciously give up the primary goal and, instead, strive for a secondary goal.* You can do this by several means. One is to build up one type of activity in place of another that has failed. A second is to shift to a more socially acceptable goal. A third is to accept the goals of others because you see that they are admired. These and other methods make it easier to deal with the frustration, because you unconsciously move away from the unachieved goals to ones that are more in your reach and, thus, can satisfy your needs.

When you use *deception* as a defense, however, *you protect yourself by fooling yourself.* You unconsciously change your perception of the threatening situation and the emotions that are involved, perhaps by building excuses, seeing another person as the culprit, logically proving to yourself that you are correct, or forgetting your thoughts or feelings. These and other methods make it possible for you to handle the frustration because you do not see yourself as the source of the problem. Rather, you end up blaming other people or external conditions.

The third major type of defense mechanism—*withdrawal*—operates in quite a different way. *It leads you to move away from the frustrating situation.* You may do this by becoming over-involved in many other activities, by withdrawing into yourself psychologically, or by creating fantasies in which you see yourself reaching your goals. None of these behaviors solves the problem; however, they do help to reduce the emotional pain accompanying the frustration.

So we see that, when your needs are threatened or unmet, you unconsciously react. Whether you react with anxiety, fear,

---

[1] The following discussion is meant to supplement the material presented in Chapter II. Therefore, before proceeding with the next section, review the discussion of unconscious factors in Chapter II.

anger, hostility, or by resorting to defense mechanisms, your reaction is bound to influence your efforts to achieve. Thus, your efforts to meet course-demands will also be influenced. I shall discuss this point shortly.

Gratification-Related Unconscious Factors

The attempt to satisfy your personality needs also brings into play unconscious reactions. In contrast to the frustration-related factors that tend to prevent close relationships with other people, these tend to facilitate such relationships. When your needs are gratified, you will feel more positive toward the people or conditions that aided in the process. In contrast to experiencing anxiety, fear, anger, or hostility, you will react with the emotions of joy, affection, or love. Instead of using defense mechanisms, you will use identification and empathy.

When your needs are gratified, or when you anticipate this satisfaction, you first experience *joy*. You have *an immediate, highly pleasant reaction;* you feel good! When another individual has helped you gain this satisfaction, you very frequently want to *carry over this feeling and express it toward the other person.* If this does occur, you are expressing *affection. When you anticipate that another person will, or when he does, satisfy your needs over a period of time, this affection typically turns to love.* As a strong feeling or attachment for another person, love represents the strongest emotional reaction to need gratification.

Although you are usually aware of feeling "good" when these emotions occur, you are not often aware of their nature or why they have occurred. At first they are unconscious factors, although later you may become aware of their presence. Even in the latter case, however, two other reactions do occur of which you are rarely aware: *identification* and *empathy.* As you experience these pleasurable emotions toward others, you will frequently *begin to accept unconsciously the purposes and values of the other person.* When this occurs you *are identifying with that person.* In other words, when you perceive that another person will, or is, satisfying your needs, you have a pleasurable emotional experience and at the same time begin to move closer to that person psychologically. You become more like that person!

Along with this process, you may also empathize with that individual. Since you feel positive toward him, *you can also understand better how he thinks and feels.* By empathizing, *you put yourself in "his shoes."* Because of this understanding, the other person typically reacts even more favorably, and this in turn leads to greater need satisfaction and more favorable emotional reactions.

Relationship to Course-Demands

We have just seen that you will probably react unconsciously in several ways when your personality needs are frustrated or gratified. You should be able to see that these reactions are related to course-demands in many ways. Since course-demands are requirements that must be met, when you attempt to meet them, your needs may be threatened, frustrated, or satisfied. When you encounter frustration, you can anticipate that you will most likely react with an emotion such as anxiety, fear, anger, or hostility and utilize one or more defense mechanisms. For example, if you fail an examination (an Activity) and you are interested in passing the course (Goal), you may become angry with the professor (anger and hostility) and explain your poor results as a result of a poor examination (deception).

In contrast, if you do very well in class recitation (an Activity), you will probably feel pleasure (joy), and you may say that this professor is "great" (affection). You may even find yourself defending his way of teaching when arguing with a friend (identification).

These examples show quite simply how unconscious factors can aid or hinder your efforts to meet course-demands. This is especially true when the demands are closely associated with the professor. As I pointed out in Chapter V, although he is instrumental in establishing all of the course-demands, he is particularly involved in the Activities, Regulations, Goals, Teacher Evaluation, and Professor's Personality. This in itself explains why your reaction to your instructor is so important in your efforts to succeed. Since these reactions are typically unconscious, they really complicate your efforts to meet course-demands.

Possible Modifications

While you probably cannot directly modify your unconscious factors, you can become more alert to their presence. In view of the above discussion, you should now realize that any great modifications require professional help. However, the efforts of a professional to help you may take considerable time. In the meantime, you may have to drop the course, work at it but anticipate poor results, or plan to take it from another instructor whose course-demands you can meet. Your decision, of course, depends upon your other self-demands. If your goals are not threatened by this course, you may decide to plug along, even though you anticipate doing poorly. However, your need for achievement may be so strong that you will have to drop it.

PERSONALITY NEEDS

Because most of us are unaware of our personality needs, it is also extremely difficult to modify them. In addition, the biological ones are very dependent upon genetic background. Even if you wanted to, you could not eliminate your needs for food, water, activity, or sex. The most you can do is to modify the ways in which you try to gratify them. Similarly, because most of your psychological needs have evolved over a long period of time, changing them is also extremely difficult. Another problem is that, because of their nature, when you ignore them their

demand for satisfaction becomes stronger, and therefore you tend to end up satisfying them. This, in turn, perpetuates their existence.

Because of these difficulties, there are very few alternatives available if you desire to modify this self-demand. In fact, the same ones that were identified for unconscious factors can be used with personality needs. Thus, you can (1) ignore them, (2) try to be alert to their presence, and (3) get help in understanding them. In order to facilitate the last two, I shall now discuss in more detail the nature of personality needs. They will be grouped as biological and psychological needs.[2]

Biological Personality Needs

Throughout your life you will be trying to satisfy essentially the same biological needs. From infancy on, in order to maintain a physiological balance, you must meet the need for *food, water, air, activity, elimination,* and *sleep.* From early adolescence on, you must also satisfy the mature sexual need. Although these needs are constantly with you, you have little control over them. Their intensity increases and decreases primarily because of natural body conditions. As you get older, however, you become more aware of their rhythm and can also put off their gratification for longer time periods.

Because the sex need becomes so powerful during the college-age years, I should say a bit more about its impact on your behavior. With the onset of puberty (sexual maturing), the satisfaction of this need will tend to dominate your behavior. Although the other biological needs still must be satisfied, much of your time and energy, consciously and unconsciously, will probably be spent in satisfying this need. In fact, at times you may temporarily forego the satisfaction of your needs

[2] The following discussion is meant to supplement the material presented in Chapter II. Therefore, before proceeding with the next section, review the discussion of personality needs in Chapter II.

for food and sleep in your efforts to reduce this striving.

Although this need is very strong, you have probably been taught certain cultural values and attitudes that restrict the ways in which you can satisfy this need. As a result, you may not be able to satisfy this need directly or fully. As with any frustration, various emotions become involved and you will use certain defense mechanisms. Because these reactions are typically unconscious, you are not aware of the connection between the frustration of this need and your behavior. I shall discuss this point shortly when looking at the relationship between needs and course-demands.

Psychological Personality Needs

Although you can at times be aware of your biological needs, this is typically not true of psychological needs. Whereas you can sense hunger, thirst, and the need for elimination and can name them as such, you may not be able to identify your non-biological strivings. Instead, you pinpoint goals. In place of say-

ing, "I have a strong achievement need," you say, "I want to get a college degree." Instead of saying, "I have a strong dominance need," you say, "I want to be elected chairman."

Although authorities do not completely agree on the number and the nature of psychological needs, there is general agreement about certain common ones. I have listed in Figure 20 ten of these, along with their definitions. As you study this list, you should remember that you probably possess most of these needs to some extent, that the needs have evolved over a long period of time, and that usually you will not know when they are functioning.

Relationship to Course-Demands

Because some personality needs are always seeking satisfaction, your behavior is always influenced in some way by these needs. This means that your efforts to meet course-demands are always affected by your biological or psychological needs. In fact, your desire to meet course-demands is itself a result of your needs! Let's see how this princi-

Figure 20 • TEN COMMON PSYCHOLOGICAL PERSONALITY NEEDS*

Need	Definition
1. Abasement	To submit passively to external force. To accept injury, blame, criticism, punishment. To become resigned to fate.
2. Achievement	To accomplish something difficult. To rival and surpass others.
3. Affiliation	To seek out and enjoy close and cooperative relationships with other people. To adhere and remain loyal to a friend.
4. Counteraction	To master and make up for a failure by renewed striving. To overcome weaknesses. To maintain self-respect and pride on a high level.
5. Deference	To admire and support a superior. To yield readily to the influence of others. To conform to custom.
6. Exhibition	To make an impression. To be seen and heard. To excite, entertain, shock, or entice others.
7. Nurturance	To give sympathy to and gratify the needs of weak and helpless persons. To feed, help, support, console, protect, nurse.
8. Order	To put things in order. To achieve cleanliness, arrangement, balance, neatness, and precision.
9. Succorance	To have one's needs gratified by the sympathetic aid of another person. To be nursed, supported, protected, loved, guided, forgiven, consoled.
10. Understanding	To ask or answer general questions. To be interested in theory. To speculate, formulate, analyze, and generalize.

* Reprinted by permission of Alfred A. Knopf, Inc., from *Elements of Psychology* by David Kretch and Richard S. Crutchfield. Copyright, © 1962 by David Kretch and Richard S. Crutchfield.

ple can apply to your biological needs. If you are attempting to complete an assigned term paper (an Activity and Regulation), your need for sleep may be so overpowering that you cannot concentrate. You may even become so groggy that you cannot see clearly. Finally, you may fall asleep, leaving the paper unfinished.

We can also see the same relationship between your behavior and your sexual need, although in this instance it may be more indirect. If you are preparing for an examination (an Activity and Regulation) to be taken on Monday, and you are planning to attend a weekend dance, you anticipated sexual gratification may interfere with your efforts to study. (This gratification can be through direct sexual behavior or indirect social behavior with members of the opposite sex.) Although you may not consciously think about the dance, you may daydream about it and the pleasure you will experience. Although you try to concentrate on your studies, you may discover that you have to call your friend to discuss the coming dance. Altogether you may spend very little time in study that weekend!

We can also see that your psychological needs have a great deal of influence. If you have a strong need for achievement, for example, this need can help you overcome course-demands that do not completely fit your other self-demands. This may occur when your goals are different from the goals of a course. Despite this difference, your overall need to succeed may be strong enough to lead you to study hard, even though you are not interested in the course.

A contrary result may occur because of another need. If you have a strong need for autonomy and your professor requires conformity (Professor's Personality), you may rebel against this instructor and his course. As a result, you may unconsciously refuse to do the assignments well or unconsciously react with hostility and use the defense mechanism of withdrawal. Neither of these

reactions will help you in your efforts to succeed.

Despite the simplicity of the above examples, personality needs typically have multiple and complex relationships with course-demands. Since you are seeking to satisfy several needs simultaneously, these efforts may help you to meet certain course-demands but hinder others. For example, your strong need for achievement may help, while your need for autonomy may hinder.

Possible Modifications

The above example points up well the difficulties in modifying this self-demand. If the multiplicity of your needs is coupled with the fact they are usually unconscious, it is not surprising if you cannot, by yourself, consciously modify them. The best that you can do is to become somewhat aware of their presence. Then, through professional help, some modifications may be possible. As with other Unconscious Factors, however, if your needs are inconsistent with the course-demands, you may have to accept a lower level of achievement, drop the course, or take it from another instructor.

ATTITUDES

In comparison to these two self-demands, some attitudes are less difficult to modify. Nevertheless, most attitudes tend to resist change for several reasons. First, as I indicated in Chapter II, you are unaware of many of your attitudes. Second, many attitudes develop in emotional situations such as the family. Third, when your attitudes are challenged, you typically react emotionally. Finally, many of your attitudes have developed over a long time period.

Despite their general resistance to change, attitudes vary widely in their ability to be modified. Those attitudes which are not unconscious, have not developed in highly emotional situations, and are of recent origin are the most subject to change. These may include attitudes toward certain school sub-jects, certain occupations, certain social groups, or certain leisure activities. In con-trast, attitudes toward authority, religion, work, or education may be less changeable; they probably began to evolve in early child-hood and have been solidified over time. Notice also that these are attitudes toward general, abstract ideas, whereas the former are attitudes toward specific aspects of broad categories.

Because of these differences, several al-ternatives are available to you in your efforts to modify this self-demand. In addition to the three mentioned for Unconscious Factors (ignoring them, becoming more aware of their presence, and getting professional help in understanding them), there are two other courses of action possible: (1) analyzing them carefully, and (2) making a conscious effort to change them. Thus, you can become more aware of the nature of some of your attitudes and, once you have done this, carry out behaviors to modify them. I have already briefly discussed how you can become more aware of your attitudes. After discussing in more detail the various kinds of attitudes and their relationship to course-demands, I shall discuss how they can be modified.[3]

Significant Attitudes and Their Relationship to Course-Demands

As I have pointed out, you develop attitudes toward numerous ideas, people, groups, con-ditions, and events. In this section I shall dis-cuss attitudes that are particularly signifi-cant during the adolescent and college years. One of the most crucial is the attitude toward *authority: this refers to the way you view people in authority positions.* These may be teachers, policemen, supervisors, and so on. This attitude typically evolves in childhood, and it is very much influenced by the type of

parental upbringing you have experienced. Because of your background, you may de-velop a positive or negative attitude in your early years that will carry over to college age. If you develop a negative attitude, your im-mediate, spontaneous (frequently uncon-scious) reaction is to distrust any authority figure. You may also become anxious and threatened. As you grow up, your further experiences with authority figures will cause you either to continue to hold the attitude you have learned or to modify it. Your ex-periences with numerous teachers will be very influential by the time you reach college age.

I am sure you can see the tremendous importance that this attitude may have for you. As you attempt to meet course-demands that are very much influenced by your pro-fessor (an authority figure), you may imme-diately and unconsciously react, negatively or positively. Before the first week of a course has passed, your attitude toward authority will be affecting your behavior. If you have a generally positive attitude, you will tend to react positively to him. You will try to meet his demands. However, if the opposite is true, you will tend to resist him, become anxious, and may even begin to use defense mechanisms. If this is the case, your chances of meeting the other course-demands are very poor.

Attitudes toward *schooling* are also very significant: *this refers to your general disposi-tion toward going to school.* This attitude also depends to a large extent on early pa-rental teachings; however, it is further devel-oped by your experiences during the elemen-tary, junior high, and senior high school years. You can develop a positive attitude, so that you look forward to attending and par-ticipating in the activities of a college. With this kind of attitude, you will automatically react with pleasure when you think about your school years—past, present, and future. If you have a negative attitude, you will tend to resist the thought of going to college.

---

[3] The following discussion is meant to supplement the material presented in Chapter II. Therefore, before proceeding with the next section, review the discussion of attitudes in Chapter II.

You may understand the necessity for getting a college degree, but you do not look forward to more academic experiences. College becomes a necessary evil!

There should be no question about the relationship of this attitude to course-demands. If you possess a positive attitude toward schooling, it will make you feel favorable, at first, toward all courses. It will lead you to approach Activities and Regulations with pleasure. Should you have a negative attitude, however, it will be especially difficult to overcome: you will begin each course with some dread—one more necessary evil to get out of the way. Such a beginning will make it difficult for you to expend any extra efforts to meet the course-demands. Instead, you will probably find initial failure, which will frustrate you and, in turn, will bring into play your defense mechanisms—which may prevent you from gaining your desired success.[4] Thus, a whole chain reaction can result from an initial negative attitude.

A closely related area is the attitude toward *study*. If you have a positive attitude toward schooling, you generally have a positive attitude toward study: *the latter refers to your willingness to carry out behaviors directed at gaining academic success.* However, as I mentioned in Chapter III, you may have various reasons for going to college. Thus, you may be positive about schooling because it fits your desire for athletic or social success. If this is so, you can feel positive toward college without feeling positive toward study.

As with attitudes toward authority and schooling, your attitudes toward study are very much influenced by your early family and school experiences. A positive attitude will probably result from favorable experiences in your earlier attempts to gain aca-

demic success. If your parents praised you and you gained the success you desired through study, you will tend to view these activities favorably. A negative attitude will result from opposite experiences. If you have found failure and frustration when you attempted to study, you will gradually come to look at reading, writing, memorizing, and discussing as unfavorable tasks.

The relationship of this attitude to course-demands is obvious. Since you cannot meet most Activities and Regulations without study, your study attitude has a direct and powerful effect. If you are favorably disposed toward these tasks, you will approach them with the view that they are an important part of the course. If not, you will view study as an imposition that you must perform to meet your goals—some necessary medicine to cure your ills! This type of attitude, even if you possess high abilities, will make meeting the course-demands tiresome and tedious.

Your attitude toward *work* is also important, but it is not as directly related to meeting course-demands as the previous three. *Work attitudes refer to the way in which you view the labor involved in an occupation.* You can view such activities as worthwhile, important, and invaluable in themselves or see labor as simply a means to earning a living. Further, you can see labor as a healthy mental and physical activity or as a necessary, but tiresome and distasteful, part of life.

Your attitudes toward work are also very much influenced by your family experiences. You have learned from your parents how each of them view the father's occupation as well as the mother's home responsibilities. School personnel are also important. They communicate through classroom lessons, materials, and behaviors their views of work. By the time you reach college age, your attitudes toward work are well developed.

The connections between this attitude and course-demands are indirect. The way you view work will have some effect on your reasons for going to college. If you think of

---

[4] The one exception to this principle occurs when a student has such a strong personality need to achieve that this initial frustration brings into play his defense mechanism of substitution. This leads him to try harder to make up for the initial failure. However, if his second efforts do not succeed, other defenses will be used that may prevent the desired success.

work as primarily a means to an end (to earn money), one of your main reasons for attending college is probably to gain economic success. If the college's goals do not emphasize this, you will probably not meet this self-demand. There is another more direct relationship. If you tend to view the labor involved in an occupation as tiresome and distasteful, you probably will view the labor (study) involved in your work as a student (occupation) in the same manner. In other words, your attitudes toward work and study are very closely related, since study is simply one form of labor. A negative work attitude is bound to make meeting Activities and Regulations a difficult task.

A related but somewhat different factor is your attitude toward *occupational choice: this refers to the way you view selecting an occupation and the importance it has for you.* Because you must usually choose an occupation during the college years, your attitude toward this is very important. You can have an attitude of indifference or of great concern; you can view this as something which occurs through natural processes or by deliberate, reasoned methods.

Your parents, through their behavior and example, may have put pressure on you to make a choice. Their efforts may have been reinforced by schoolteachers, counselors, and others; in addition, friends, newspapers, magazines, and television may have stressed the desirability of making an early and well thought out choice.

In response to these or other influences, your present attitude has evolved, and it is related to your course-demands. If you are anxious to make a choice (or have already done so), this choice has probably influenced your reasons for going to college. As we saw above, your reason may or may not coincide with your college's Reasons and Goals. Further, your attitude may also influence your reactions to courses that are primarily theoretical or practical. If you want to make an occupational choice, you probably prefer courses that can help you make this choice;

on the other hand, if you are not concerned about your choice, you will be freer to meet the course-demands of various types of subjects.

Another important attitude concerns interpersonal relationships. Although your attitude toward your *peers* is not as directly related to course-demands as the above-mentioned attitudes, it can affect your behavior significantly while you are in college. *This attitude refers to the way you view other students attending college.* You may value them highly, seek out their friendship, and conform to their values. In contrast, you may regard other students as competitors, avoid any close relationships, and ignore their views.

Attitudes such as these have evolved primarily as a result of your earlier experiences with others. In addition to the influence of your parents and teachers, your reactions to your peers when you were younger have largely molded your present views. If they treated you fairly and with affection, you probably have developed positive attitudes. If you encountered frustration at their hands, you probably have moved away from close relationships.

There are several connections between this attitude and your course-demands. One has to do with Reasons and Goals. You can see that an extremely positive peer attitude may lead you to place social success over academic success. In this case, you may not satisfy a course's Reasons and Goals. Such an attitude may also lead you to ignore certain Activities and Regulations in favor of associating with peers. In contrast, a negative peer attitude may cause you to be out of touch with your fellow students and thus not perceive Student Pressure. As a result, you will not be able to meet this course-demand.

One final area of importance regarding attitudes should be discussed here. Your attitudes toward *sex and marriage* can also be significant; *this attitude refers to the way you think and feel about sexual gratification and its relationship to marriage.* Although closely related to peer atttiudes, it is usually a more unconscious one. As I pointed out in the discussion of personality needs, the sex need becomes so strong during late adolescence that your attitude toward it will greatly influence your behavior. You can view it as healthy or "dirty," natural or artificial. Your efforts to satisfy it before marriage can be thought of as proper or improper. Your attitude has probably evolved to some extent from family experiences, church teachings, and peer relationships. By college age, your friends have also established sexual guidelines that you probably accept or modify.

The relationship between your sexual and marriage attitudes and course-demands can be direct or indirect. These attitudes can influence the type of goals you establish. Without realizing it, you may be attending college largely because of your desire to get married. This, in turn, may indirectly be stimulated by a need for sexual gratification which you feel can be accomplished only through marriage. Such a goal may lead to behavior that will prevent you from meeting the other course-demands.

Your sexual attitude can also directly influence your academic achievement in certain courses. If your views on sexual gratification differ from those developed in a biology, psychology, or religion course, you may find that you cannot successfully carry out the required Activities. For example, your attitude may interfere with your ability to write a term paper or answer an exam question dealing with this topic. As a result, you will be unable to meet this course-demand.

Possible Attitude Modifications

In view of the above discussion, it should be very clear now that attitudes vary widely in their ability to be modified. Whereas your attitudes toward authority and sex are probably most difficult to change, your attitudes toward study and occupational choice should be least difficult to change. Even the latter two, however, because they have evolved over a considerable period of time, tend to resist modification, but the fact that you can become more aware of these attitudes facilitates your efforts.

But what can you do to become more aware of your attitudes? Certainly, as I mentioned earlier, awareness is an important step in the process of consciously changing attitudes. Fortunately, there are several ways of becoming aware of your attitudes. As I noted in Chapter VI, you can use your Self, Non-School Experiences, Significant Others, and College Personnel as sources for understanding your attitudes. You can consider how you react to the various authority figures whom you encounter, in and out of the educational setting. You can compare your perceptions with those of other people. Furthermore, for certain attitudes, especially toward schooling, study, and work, you can take attitude inventories or tests that can tell you how your attitudes compare with those of other adolescents. You can ask your counselor about taking one or more of these inventories; at the end of this chapter I have listed the names of two which may be helpful.

In addition to getting more information, three other conditions must exist in order for you to change your attitudes. First, you must practice behaviors directed at changing an attitude; second, you must receive acceptance from others in your efforts to change; third, you must receive pleasure in the process of changing. Let me explain each of these points. If you know you have a negative attitude toward schooling—you view it as a necessary evil—you must carry out behaviors directed at producing a favorable attitude. Instead of staying away from classes, you must attend them; instead of seeing little value in the courses, you must try to think of possible values; instead of not doing assignments, you must perform them as soon as possible. In other words, you must carry out behaviors that represent a favorable attitude.

However, this is not enough. While carrying out these new behaviors, others (your teachers, peers, parents, girl friend, and so on) will have to show that they like your new behaviors. If they ignore your class attendance or your completed assignments, you will soon revert to your old ways. Through their attention and recognition, however, you can gain enough pleasure to carry you over during the changing state, until you gain pleasure from the new behaviors themselves. When this last point is reached, that is, when going to classes is itself pleasurable, your attitude toward schooling will then be favorable.

Thus, one very important point about changing attitudes is that you cannot change your attitudes by yourself. Their modification is to a great extent dependent upon the actions of others. Thus, your efforts to change your attitudes can end in failure. Furthermore, you now can see that you should attempt to change your attitudes only at a time when you anticipate positive reactions from others. For example, you should try to modify a negative schooling attitude when you have a teacher whom you either like or antici-

pate liking. To attempt to change with a teacher you dislike is likely to lead only to failure.

CHAPTER SUMMARY

We have seen that modifying self-demands involves certain difficulties. You may not realize that you have a self-demand; in addition, changing it may involve considerable emotion. Since most self-demands evolve over a long period of time, this may also prohibit change.

Despite these difficulties, there are some ways of modifying them. In this chapter we looked at the most difficult ones to change and discussed possible means of modifying them. For all three—unconscious factors, personality needs, and attitudes—determining their nature is the most important step. Beginning here, I have discussed each in considerable detail and then offered practical suggestions for changing each.

THOUGHT QUESTIONS

1. Why is it more difficult to modify self-demands that involve considerable emotion than those that are largely rational in nature? How can this emotional component be dealt with?
2. Is it really possible for a student to gain a better understanding of his unconscious factors? Why do you say this?
3. Which frustration-related unconscious factors seem to be the most difficult to change? Why?
4. Which psychological personality needs are probably the easiest to modify? Why?
5. How could you modify one of your negative attitudes? Which of your personality needs might interfere with your attempts? Why?

SELECTED REFERENCES

Unconscious Factors

Heyns, Roger W. *The Psychology of Personal Adjustment.* New York: Dryden Press, 1958. Chapters 1, 4, 6.

Lindgren, Henry C. *Psychology of Personal and Social Adjustment,* rev. ed. New York: American, 1959. Chapter 1.

Voeks, Virginia. *On Becoming an Educated Person,* rev. ed. Philadelphia: Saunders, 1964. Chapter 4.

Wattenberg, William W. *The Adolescent Years.* New York: Harcourt Brace, 1955. Chapter 24.

Personality Needs

Daly, Sheila J. *Questions Teen-Agers Ask.* New York: Dodd Mead, 1963. Chapters 9–10.

Lazarus, Richard S. *Adjustment and Personality.* New York: McGraw-Hill, 1961. Chapter 2.

Menninger, William C. *Growing Up Emotionally.* Chicago: Science Research Associates, 1960. Chapter 1–8.

Senick, Daniel. *Your Personality and Your Job.* Chicago: Science Research Associates, 1960. Chapter 5.

Attitudes

Dudycha, George J. *Learn More with Less Effort.* New York: Harper, 1957. Chapter 7.

Fisher, M. B., and Noble, J. L. *College Education As Personal Development.* Englewood Cliffs: Prentice-Hall, 1960.

Garrison, Roger H. *The Adventure of Learning in College.* New York: Harper, 1959. Chapters 3, 5, 8, 10, 12.

Attitude Inventories

Allport, Vernon, and Lindzey, Gardner. *Study of Values,* rev. ed. Boston: Houghton Mifflin, 1960.

Brown, W. H., and Holtzman, W. F. *Survey of Study Habits and Attitudes.* New York: The Psychological Corporation, 1953.

CHAPTER IX

Habits, Reasons, and Goals

WE SHALL NOW LOOK AT THE SELF-DEMANDS that are moderately difficult to modify, using the same approach that we used in the previous chapter.

HABITS

In comparison to attitudes, most habits are easier to modify. As I indicated earlier, however, certain habits that are very influenced by personality needs and unconscious factors are difficult to change. Likewise, those habits that have existed for a long period of time can be modified only with considerable effort. In general, however, because you can become aware of most of your mental, social, or physical habits, you can carry out behaviors that will lead to their modification.

As a result, you might guess that there are several alternatives available to you. In addition to your own efforts to become alert to their presence, you can get help from others in understanding them. You can also consciously analyze them as well as consciously attempt to change them. Changing your habits, in contrast to your attitudes, is typically not so dependent upon the actions of others. Before discussing in more detail the ways that changes can be made, I will at this point describe the various kinds of habits and their relationship to course-demands.[1] This should facilitate your understanding of the procedures you will need to follow regarding your habits.

Important Habits and Their Relationship to Course-Demands

As I noted in Chapter II, we can group habits as essentially mental, social, or physical. Because there is such a wide variety of mental habits, I shall discuss here only those that seem to be most important to your academic success. These would include habitual ways of using your mental abilities and types of learning. Whenever you develop a set way of using your abilities or using various types of learning, you have added new habits to your way of behaving. *In effect, these are study habits.* Thus, we can identify mental habits related to abilities and mental habits related to types of learning.[2]

Whenever you note that you perform a certain mental ability in the same way time after time, you have identified a *mental habit related to abilities.* Thus, if you read your assignments in the same way, regardless of the content, length, or nature of the reading material, you have identified one of your reading habits. We can say the same thing for other essential abilities such as listening, questioning, remembering, writing and speaking. If you always approach learning from the same point of view, you can say you have a *mental habit related to types of learning.* Thus, instead of selecting the most appropriate types of learning for each assignment, you will, without realizing it, use the same type of learning each time (rote, association, conscious problem-solving, or unconscious insight).

The relationship of these mental habits to course-demands should be quite clear. As

we have seen, most courses include Activities and Regulations that require the use of certain abilities and types of learning. In addition, certain professors may require you to utilize one or more abilities or types of learning not demanded in other courses. If your mental habits fit those required by the course-demands, your chances of succeeding are very high. Where they are different, because of the direct connection between these mental habits and course-demands, they must be modified. This in itself points out the tremendous importance of knowing your mental habits.

Among the various social habits, two seem most closely connected to academic success: *habits related to peer relationships,* and *habits related to authority relationships.* As you may guess, these habits are very similar to your attitudes toward your peers and authority. When these attitudes become automatic and you carry them out regardless of the particular friend or authority figure, we can say that they have become social habits. Thus, if you are automatically cordial to your peers when you meet together, you have identified one of your social habits. Similarly, if you are automatically sarcastic with authority figures when in their presence, you have identified another social habit.

As we saw with attitudes, these social habits are related to meeting course-demands. Your habitual behavior toward your peers may either hinder or help you in your efforts to understand Student Pressure. On the one hand, it may aid you in knowing these students better; while, on the other, it may create a barrier to perceiving their goals and abilities.

Your social habits toward authority figures can also influence your ability to meet course-demands. In particular, your habitual reactions to professors either may or may not help you to deal with the Professor's Personality. If you habitually (consciously or unconsciously) resist the professor's attempts to be friendly or resist his invitations to seek help through individual conferences, you will

---

[1] The following discussion is meant to supplement the material presented in Chapter II. Therefore, before proceeding with the next section, review the discussion of habits in Chapter II.

[2] If you have forgotten my discussion of the various types of learning you can use, review Chapter IV.

not obtain any better understanding of his personality. By contrast, if you automatically utilize these opportunities, you will be in a better position to meet this course-demand.

There are several physical habits that are closely related to academic success in most courses. These include habits in the *care and use of the body*. Because most college courses require intensive study that involves considerable time and energy, if you do not take care of yourself physically, the condition of your body may soon interfere with your mental activities. Certainly by the time you have reached college age, you have already developed numerous habits related to the care of your body. Practically without thinking you will brush your teeth, bathe, and eat, for example. You can prepare for bed, exercise, and rest, while preoccupied with other thoughts. However, the routine you must follow in college may be quite different from the one you followed in high school. Thus, the physical habits that helped you before may now be interfering with your attempts to maintain good physical health.

In order to carry out various course Activities and Regulations, you must be flexible in your use of your body. At times you will need to work actively for long periods in study or in the laboratory, while at other times you will need to sit passively while listening to lectures and taking notes. If you can function well only in a fixed pattern, your physical health will suffer, and this, in turn, will affect your mental processes. If you then become frustrated, your emotional responses may also upset your usual physical habits; this, in turn, can further interfere with your ability to meet the course-demands.

Modifying Habits

As we noted above, there are several methods of attempting to change habits. First, you must become aware of their existence. You will recall from Chapter VI that you can use several sources to discover your mental, social, and physical habits: these include the Self, High School Record, Non-School Activities, Test Results, Significant Others, College Personnel, and College Record. Let me elaborate a bit more on the use of these sources.

By utilizing introspective observations (using the Self), the observations of others (Significant Others and College Personnel), and an analysis of past performance (High School Record, Non-School Activities, Test Record, and College Record), you can combine primarily subjective and objective data to gain a total picture of your habits. In addition to analyzing your past activities, you must study your present behavior. One way of doing this is to keep a record of your behavior over a certain period of time. Thus, if you are interested in discovering your mental habits, you need to keep track of how you read or listen or remember. Keeping a daily log is a simple way of doing this. If this analysis displays a consistent pattern, you can conclude that you have identified one of your mental habits.

This information will then have to be checked against the observations of others. You can ask your roommate, instructor, or advisor to give you their perceptions of your mental habits. These data can then be compared with your test results (such as study-habits questionnaires), already available or obtained concurrently. Only after all of these data are analyzed and compared, can you conclude that you have identified your mental habits.

Assuming that you have now become aware of their existence, the second step in modifying habits involves your conscious efforts to change them. As I noted in Chapter II, this typically involves some pain and frustration, because your present habits evolved from ways of behaving which seemed to provide you with more pleasure than pain. Thus, in attempting to change them, you will be foregoing some pleasure. For example, even though you discover that one of your mental habits—say, reading—is not particularly helpful, you will be giving up some of the security it has provided. While attempting to change this habit, you should anticipate a certain amount of frustration. When your new reading behaviors seem to be better than the old ones, you will begin to obtain more pleasure from them, and, thus, the new habit will be created.

To accomplish this, however, you must know what behaviors you want to substitute for the established habits. If you do not have a clear idea of the desired habit, you will not be able to get beyond the initial frustration. Hence, if you want to change your reading habit, you must know other ways of reading, not in general, but in particular. You must be able to compare the specific behaviors you habitually carry out with those you want to substitute.

Once you have identified the desired behaviors, you are ready for the third step in changing habits. You must practice the new behaviors until they become satisfying and almost automatic. It is during this practice phase that you should anticipate the greatest amount of frustration. Because you are no longer gaining pleasure from the old habit and have not yet arrived at the point of receiving pleasure from the new behaviors, your reading may temporarily be worse than it was before you decided to change!

It is during this third step that the behavior of other people can be either very beneficial or detrimental to your efforts. As with changing attitudes, the pleasure you will receive if others recognize and reward your efforts to modify your behavior can carry you to the point where you receive direct satisfaction from the newly established habit. However, in contrast to attitudes, because habits are more clearly observable, we can see their step-by-step change more easily and thus receive direct satisfaction sooner than from attitude changes. Hence, even a small change in your reading habits can give you some direct pleasure, if you see that you can read faster or with greater understanding.

The final step in modifying habits is simply a continuation of step three. The newly established set of behaviors must be practiced until it becomes automatic. This is usually not difficult, since the amount of pleasure will increase as the behaviors become more habitual. In other words, the more you practice your new reading habit, the more you will discover that it produces good results. (You read faster and better.) These results themselves increase your pleasure, and this, in turn, leads you to continue the habit. Thus, a new habit has been established.

REASONS AND GOALS

Reasons and goals represent a self-demand that is quite different from the other self-demands that we have discussed thus far. As you recall from Chapters III and VI, this self-demand deals with your reasons for going to college. Before discussing possible modifications, I should point out the typical process by which you acquire your Reasons and Goals. As with most personality needs, attitudes, and habits, your reasons are very influenced by your family upbringing. To a great extent, your parents, either directly or indirectly, have shaped your thinking about going to college. From early years, many parents point out the advantages of a college education; some stress the cultural aspects, others emphasize the occupational features, while still others point up the social benefits.

Other members of your family can also significantly affect your thinking. The model of an older sister or uncle can serve as an inspiration to attend college. School personnel can also serve as inspirations, and, thus, they can influence you too. In addition, their ideas about the value of a college education probably have great meaning for you, although you may be more influenced by peers. What close friends think and feel about college probably became very important to you in the late high school years. Finally, you should not overlook the impact of the mass media in influencing your thinking. In our society today, the many values of a college education are constantly being repeated by television, radio, newspapers, and magazines. From all of these sources, then, the high school student approaches college entrance with one or more conscious reasons for going to college and probably some unconscious ones too.

Although some of your reasons may be unconscious, most are conscious and, thus, subject to modification. This means that you can become aware of most of them and can logically figure out why other reasons for going to college will help you to succeed.

Despite this generalization, there are four factors that can hinder your efforts to modify this self-demand. One is that you may be unaware of your *real* reasons for attending college. As I indicated in Chapter III, you may think you are attending college to prepare for an occupation, whereas, in reality, you may attend because you are fulfilling your parents' wishes. Another possible hindrance is that you may be emotionally committed to certain goals. In order to modify the goal, you must also be able to handle the emotions attached to that goal. Thus, if you are primarily attending college to fulfill your parents' wishes, changing this reason will require that you deal with all the emotions of love, anger, hate, or dependency which you may feel toward your parents. Since they may be difficult to deal with, it may be easier for you to keep your present reasons, even though you may want to change.

A third possible difficulty in modifying goals concerns societal pressure. Most of us have grown up in a society that encourages "sticking to a goal" until it is achieved and discourages "not finishing what you start." We have learned to feel guilty if we do not complete a task. While, in general, this "stick-to-it-ness" is a valuable trait, it can at times be detrimental. This is especially true regarding college, since most students do not really have a thorough knowledge of themselves when they decide to go to college. Thus, frequently goals are prematurely determined. After attending college a while, you are then

in a better position to establish meaningful goals. However, because of your guilt feelings, you may resist making changes.

A final reason why students have difficulty in changing their goals may be their unawareness of other possible goals. Because of your own limited family, school, and peer relationships, you may not have been exposed to different kinds of reasons for going to college. Thus, you may think that all students go to college to get a better job; you may not realize that some students attend college primarily to learn more about their cultural heritage.

From this discussion, you can see that modifying goals is affected by two factors that are not easily to subject to change and two factors that can be readily changed. The former include the emotional commitment to certain goals and the guilt encountered in thinking of changing. The latter include a lack of awareness of your real goals and a lack of awareness of other possible goals. Because of these latter two factors, there are several specific procedures available for modifying this self-demand. Before looking at these methods, let's view in more detail the kinds of Reasons and Goals you might have for going to college.[3]

Common Reasons and Goals and Their Relationship to Course-Demands

We saw in Chapter III that your Reasons and Goals with regard to going to college can be viewed as your definition of success. We also saw that these Reasons and Goals can be classified as fitting one or more types of success. Now, we can look at the six types of success desired and see the relationship of each to typical course-demands.

You will recall that when you desire a high scholastic average or a high level of scholastic learning, we can say that you desire *academic success*. Although you may

---

[3] The following discussion is meant to supplement the material presented in Chapter III. Therefore, before proceeding with the next section, review the discussion of Reasons and Goals in that chapter.

want both (a high average and learning), you may *be interested* in only one or the other. In fact, you may be confused in your own mind about the difference. Because of your background, you may be primarily concerned with getting good grades—regardless of the amount of learning which takes place, while another student may be indifferent to grades but quite concerned about what he has learned. In addition to these differences, students also vary widely in the types of scholastic learning they desire. Some may be interested in acquiring factual knowledge; others wish to develop practical vocational skills; still others prefer to develop critical thinking skills with reference to abstract material. Some other possible goals of scholastic learning are the development of the ability to synthesize ideas, of analytical reading skills, of deductive thinking, and of positive attitudes toward independent thinking.

These types of goals (as well as many more) can obviously have a very close relationship to course-demands. As you recall, one of the basic course-demands is called Goals; it is concerned with the goals of the course, as expressed in the bulletin or stated by the professor and other students. Since most course Goals heavily emphasize desired scholastic learning, your chances of succeeding are much higher if your scholastic goals are similar to those of your courses. On the other hand, if your desire for academic success is limited to getting high grades, the chances of your meeting the various Goals of the course are very low. You may gain academic success (high grades) by meeting the other course-demands (Activities and Regulations), yet not acquire certain types of scholastic learning. Thus, you may be able to remember factual knowledge for tests (Activity) but not develop any scientific attitude toward solving problems (part of the goal of the course, but not measured by tests).

If your Reasons and Goals are primarily to gain *artistic success*, there is no assurance whatsoever that you will gain academic success. You can achieve academic success along with artistic success only if the course-demands include Goals, Regulations, or Activities related to artistic expression through various media such as music, painting, sculpture, dancing, writing, or drama. As you might guess, courses in these various disciplines generally require that you develop skills in expressing yourself. Thus, courses in painting may include goals such as to develop the ability to paint in oils, to develop skill in the use of pen and ink, or to develop the ability to mix colors.

If you desire artistic success, you can probably meet the course-demands of these courses (provided you have minimum ability), although you may encounter considerable difficulty in meeting the course-demands of other courses, particularly if your Reasons and Goals do not include interest in other types of success. Thus, if you want to graduate from college, you will have to have, or develop, goals related to other types of success.

If you are interested in *occupational success*, you may, or may not, desire artistic or academic success. As I have already pointed out, some students are not primarily interested in occupational achievement. Thus, you could go to college in order to learn to express yourself artistically but be indifferent to becoming a successful, professional painter. If you also desire the latter, you will be interested in both artistic and occupational success.

When you attend college primarily for occupational reasons, you usually prefer those courses that have a direct or indirect connection with your vocational choice. For example, a student planning to become a medical doctor would be likely to prefer courses in biology, chemistry, or psychology, while a student interested in becoming a journalist would probably prefer courses in English literature, creative writing, and history. In other words, your desire for occupational success leads to your course preferences.

Therefore, there is typically a close relationship between your occupational reasons for going to college and course-demands. When the goals of a course include knowledge and skills applicable to your occupational choice, you should be better able to meet the course-demands, provided that you can carry out the necessary Activities and Regulations. Further, if a course is not concerned with practical applications and if you desire occupational success, you will probably find it uninteresting and, thus, have little desire to meet the other course-demands. Such a situation usually means that you cannot concentrate for long on the subject while studying. (Remember our friend David?) The implications for acquiring academic success should be obvious!

We have seen, in discussing academic, artistic, and occupational reasons for going to college, that they can be helpful to you as you meet many of the course-demands. Because various courses are concerned with these three types of success, a student with these goals possesses a positive factor in his efforts to complete college. On the other hand, students concerned primarily with social, athletic, or economic success will discover that many subjects have course-demands that are unrelated or contrary to these goals.

Take, for example, *social success*. If you want social success, you want to be accepted and to function well with others socially: you are striving for achievement in interpersonal relations. You want to be accepted in various groups or to succeed with others individually. In the latter category, you may desire success with the opposite sex and a relationship leading to marriage. It should be quite clear to you that very few, if any, college courses are concerned with these goals. Although some may want you to become aware of the ways in which groups operate and the problems of marriage, they are typically not concerned with the practical application of these concepts to the students. The extracurricular program and student personnel services are more interested in these practical aspects.

This is also true of *athletic success*. Not even physical education courses have, as their primary goal, the development of outstanding players in a sport. This aim may exist, but it usually falls outside the regular curriculum. Except in those colleges where varsity athletes are given special academic consideration, if you are seeking athletic success, you will find your goals are not consistent with most course-demands.

This is likewise true if you are primarily concerned with *economic* success. An economic goal means that you want to earn or accumulate enough money to purchase the goods and services you desire, regardless of the manner by which you do this. Your goal is wealth, and you will do whatever is necessary to acquire it. (Naturally, your own values will determine whether you will go outside the law to reach this goal.) When you strongly believe that acquiring economic success can be achieved by going to college, this goal may aid you to meet various course-demands that are not similar to your goal. However, because finishing college is a long and difficult process, this initial reason alone will probably not be powerful enough to carry you along. The other course-demands will probably be too different for you to meet them for more than a short period of time.

In addition to wanting to achieve one or more of these six types of success, you may have come to college because of other reasons that are even less related to course-demands. We can group these reasons under the heading "pressures from others"; these can include family, peer, and general societal pressures. I have indicated above that your family can have a very powerful influence on your reasons for going to college. In addition to helping shape specific reasons, they can create an overall pressure to attend college. Many parents today impress upon their children the need to go to college so strongly that the student automatically assumes that he will go but does almost no thinking about why he is going. He knows, however, that college is a "must." Although this strong desire to go to college is not in itself harmful, it can be detrimental when, desiring to please your parents, you go only because they want you to do so.

Pressure from peers can be just as powerful, but it usually operates in a different way. During the late high school years, friends frequently talk about post-high school plans. Because the adolescent is very much influenced by the opinions of his peers, their views about college become extremely important to him. If his close friends are planning to go to college, he will probably want to go too. It doesn't matter whether they know why they are going, or what they plan to study. Frequently he describes his reasons for going this way: "All my friends are going. If I didn't go, I'd be left out of everything."

To go to college for this reason may be satisfying to you but it is not particularly related to meeting course-demands. It would be difficult, indeed, to find a single course that concludes as a Goal a desire to help the student be with his friends! Because of this inconsistency, this type of reason rarely helps you complete your college program, although you may gain social success in this manner.

In addition to pressures from the family and peers, there is a general societal pressure which may have led you to go to college. In our country, there is current a widely held belief that, in order to succeed, you must have a college education. This idea is expressed in different ways: sometimes you are told that you will earn much more money if you go to college; that you will be able to select the kind of job you want; that you will develop the kind of associations that will help you later; and that a college education can't hurt anyone. *While these ideas may be generally true, for particular students, for you, they may be completely false!* Nevertheless, after constantly hearing these arguments from various sources—radio, television, magazines, movies, school personnel—you may conclude that you must try to go to college because everyone says it's important. For some, this turns out to be the dominant rea-

son for starting college. Such a vague reason, of course, has little relationship to specific course-demands, and, as a result, you soon discover that you have no real interest in your subjects but that you still want a "college education." This lack of interest sooner or later will probably interfere with your completion of the various Activities and Regulations that make up the course-demands. You may discover that you are faced with the problem of being unable to concentrate on your studying. While societal pressure can help you get to college, it does not help you very much in meeting your course-demands.

Modifying Reasons and Goals

In the above section, I have described how some of your reasons for going to college are, or are not, related to course-demands. Fortunately, there are several procedures that you can follow if you desire to change this self-demand. These include: (1) becoming aware of your existing Reasons and Goals in attending college; (2) becoming aware of how you acquired these Reasons and Goals; (3) becoming aware of other possible Reasons and Goals; (4) consciously setting up new Reasons and Goals; (5) consciously striving to reach the new Goals; (6) getting reactions from others as to whether you are *actually* trying to reach the new Goals; and (7) reassessing, after a period of time, your newly established Reasons and Goals. Let's look at each of these steps in more detail.

Most students can become more aware of their present Reasons and Goals for attending college. The main procedure for doing this is careful observation. Furthermore, we have already seen in Chapters III and VI that the observations of others can also be used. You will recall that you made an analysis of your Reasons using various sources of data. Throughout this process you had to look at your behavior and see if it implied any Reasons and Goals. In retrospect, however, you should now understand that you may not have identified all of the significant Reasons. With your increased knowledge of your personality needs, you can probably add one or two more to your list of reasons why you are going to college.

This shows clearly that you must constantly attempt to understand your Reasons. You cannot assume that you have completed this task after you have done it once; as you learn more about yourself through courses, new experiences, and self-analysis, what you thought to be your Reasons may no longer exist. Unless you are aware of these changes, you cannot determine whether your current Goals fit the course-demands.

The second step in changing your Goals is not quite as easy as the first. Although you may be able to determine where some of your Reasons come from, you should not expect to be able to figure out all of the sources. As I pointed out above, your Reasons may be due to the influences of others whom you were in contact with during early childhood. In this instance you may be unable to identify the source. Despite this possibility, you should be able to understand the recent influences of your parents, friends, teachers, or others. Once you have determined this, you should be able to figure out fairly accurately the kind and degree of emotional involvement in your current Goals. When there is strong involvement with these significant others, you should anticipate more difficulty in changing your Reasons and Goals.

When there is not a great deal of emotional involvement, carrying out step three should have real value. By becoming aware of other possible Reasons and Goals, you have a basis for setting up new ones to take the place of the existing ones. This awareness can develop from reading the college bulletin, books about students who have gone to college, and other references that describe colleges (see the list of references at the end of Chapter III). New ideas can also come from talking with other students, members of the faculty, other college personnel, and other adults who have finished college and are working full-time. Keeping a written rec-

ord of these various ideas should prove helpful whenever you wonder about why you are going to college.

The fourth step, consciously setting up new Reasons and Goals, is dependent upon the above procedure. Once you become aware of other possible Goals, you can logically and consciously establish a new set of Goals. Although this may sound easy, the difficult part is identifying a new goal that you can probably reach and that has real meaning to you. Thus, you can establish the Goal of becoming an outstanding historian; however, if you do not have exceptional intellectual ability, and if history is of only fleeting interest to you, such a Goal would be inappropriate.

This points out another aspect of establishing new Goals. You must realize that it is perfectly normal, and probably beneficial, to establish Goals, test yourself regarding these Goals, and then *change* to new Goals. This process incorporates the fifth step: consciously striving to reach the new Goals. If your Goal is to become an historian, you must take history courses and strive for learning and high achievement. If such behavior produces learning and achievement, the chances are quite good that this new Goal will become part of your main reasons for going to college. On the other hand, if you state this as a Goal but never take history courses, the chances are that it will never become one of your *real* Goals. In this instance, you may fool yourself into believing it is a Goal (defense mechanism), and, as a result, you may be unaware of your true Reasons.

The sixth step should also tell you if you are really striving for this newly-established Goal. Getting reactions from others can act as a check on your observations of your own behavior. For example, you may sign up for a history course and thus conclude that you want to become an historian. However, if, after a short period of time, your roommate points out that you rarely study the history assignments and that you fall asleep in history class, this information should throw some new light on your real Goals. Such behavior implies that becoming an historian is no longer a real Goal.

Such a development points out the last step in changing this self-demand. You must reassess, after a period of time, your newly established Reasons and Goals. If your behavior is directed toward achieving a Goal, you can be sure that the new Goal has become part of your self-demands. If not, you must attempt to determine again your existing Reasons and Goals.

This discussion should make it clear that Reasons and Goals, as a self-demand, are subject to modification. In fact, as you have already seen, it is only when there are strong emotional ties that changing your Reasons and Goals becomes difficult. You can expect to change your Goals, in contrast to unconscious factors, personality needs, attitudes, and habits, during your college years. The important thing is that you make such changes consciously, so that you can then determine whether the Goals will meet the course-demands.

CHAPTER SUMMARY

Various mental, social, and physical habits have been discussed in this chapter, and we have seen that they can be identified by using various procedures. Changing them involves substituting new habits by systematic practice.

After explaining why changing Reasons and Goals may prove difficult, I have discussed the relationship of this self-demand to course-demands. This has led to an analysis of the ways in which Reasons and Goals can be modified. Since you can consciously substitute other reasons and discover if you are actually striving to achieve the new goals, changing this self-demand is generally possible.

THOUGHT QUESTIONS

1. In general, why are habits more difficult to change than reasons and goals?
2. Which kind of goals are easiest to modify? Why?
3. To what extent do your Reasons and Goals meet your course-demands? How can you modify them so that they fit the course-demands better? Do you think you can make these changes? Why?
4. Which of your mental habits do not fit your course-demands? Do you think these are modifiable? Why?
5. Assuming that you are able to change these habits, will this affect your self-demand concerning attitudes? Why?

SELECTED REFERENCES

Modifying Habits

Coleman, J. C., and others. *Success in College.* Chicago: Scott Foresman, 1960. Chapter 3.

Lass, Abraham H. *How to Prepare for College.* New York: David White Co., 1962. Chapter 7.

Morgan, Clifford T., and Deese, James. *How to Study.* New York: McGraw-Hill, 1957. Chapter 2.

Modifying Reasons and Goals

Garrison, Roger H. *The Adventure of Learning in College.* New York: Harper, 1959. Chapters 4, 12, 13.

Heyns, Roger W. *The Psychology of Personal Adjustment.* New York: Dryden Press, 1958. Chapter 15.

Wattenberg, William W. *The Adolescent Years.* New York: Harcourt Brace, 1955. Chapters 2, 16.

CHAPTER X

Abilities: Reading, Listening, and Questioning

You recall that I discussed the nature of abilities in Chapter IV. At that time I also helped you compare the mental, physical, and social abilities which you possess with those required by your college. This comparison was further developed in Chapter VI.[1] In view of this, I shall concentrate here on those *mental abilities* that are required by most courses: these include reading, listening, questioning, remembering, writing, speaking, problem-solving, integrating, and creating.

Before looking at each of these mental

abilities and the ways of modifying them, I want to point out why most of them, compared to other self-demands, are easier to change: (1) you can become aware of your level of ability; (2) you can logically determine your weakness; (3) you can logically determine what changes are necessary; and (4) you can practice the desired changes. In other words, most abilities are subject to logical analysis and conscious remediation.

Likewise, you can anticipate that some abilities will be very difficult to change. This occurs when (1) they are very much based on emotion, or (2) they are dependent upon genetically determined factors. Because abili-

---

[1] Before proceeding with this section, you should review Chapters IV and VI. In this way, the material presented here will have more meaning for you.

ties are developed in different family, school, and peer situations, you can expect that various people's abilities will show different degrees of emotional involvement. As a result, you cannot accurately predict whether an ability can be easily changed, unless you know the degree of emotional involvement present as the ability was being developed.

You can, however, estimate quite well the probable chances of change if you know that the ability is primarily dependent upon biologically inherited factors. In this case, there is little chance of modification. Thus, your ability to solve highly abstract, three-dimensional mathematical problems is not too subject to significant change.

Fortunately, most of the above-mentioned abilities do not fit in these categories. Although most of them are probably in part emotionally based, and all are in part genetically determined, most have evolved largely due to environmental conditions. Thus, with effort, new environmental conditions can modify them. This is where your efforts at analysis and practice come in. Let us then turn to reading, listening, and questioning; I shall discuss these abilities in some detail, point out their relationships to course-demands, and explain how they can be modified.

READING

Nature of Reading

Perhaps the first question you should look at is, "What is reading?" Although this seems to be a fairly simple question, I think you will discover that the answer is quite complex. Pause for a minute here and think over in your own mind a possible answer to this question. Is reading getting information from a book? Or does reading occur when you look up ideas? or when you enjoy finding out what an author has written? There are many possible answers you could give.

For our purposes, a general answer to the question might go something like this: *Reading is the process of carrying on a conversa-* *tion with an author.* Now this may appear to be a rather unusual definition. Let us analyze it in a little detail. If we say that reading is the process of carrying on a conversation with an author, we mean that you, the person doing the reading, are doing about the same thing that you do when you *talk* to another person while carrying on a conversation. The major difference is that reading is a completely mental process and that you do not (normally) use your voice in this process. Instead of using oral communication, you use written symbols to carry on the conversation between the reader and the author. However, it becomes a conversation only when there is a two-way communication process between you and the writer. In other words, reading is an active process. I shall have more to say about this in the following pages.

Looking at reading as a process of conversation, we need to ask here, "What are the necessary tools to achieve this process?" I am sure you can mention some. For example, you need physical tools, such as your eyes. In addition, you need certain psychological tools: these include vocabulary, background experience, certain kinds of learning ability, various types of motivation, and other skills which we shall discuss below. In other words, just as carrying on a verbal communication with a friend requires certain kinds of tools, including your throat, your larynx, your ears, and eyes, likewise, reading requires certain tools.

Of course, you can carry on the process of reading for many different purposes. Perhaps I might list a few here. You can read to obtain information which you may use as a basis for new learning, for enjoyment itself, and to solve problems. Perhaps when you attempted to define reading earlier, you were thinking of reading as primarily a way of obtaining information. If you did, you probably ignored the active process involved. If you read to obtain information, and the information is composed mostly of facts, the main process that you go through is simply one of looking for particular facts. On the other hand, most college courses require reading which is of a different sort. You have to use reading material in college as a basis for new learning and, to a great extent, in problem-solving. To accomplish these two goals, reading as an active process becomes especially important.

A comparison of reading to a conversation with one of your friends might help to explain the above statement. Imagine that you have been talking to one of your friends. If you asked her for some information, for example, the time of day, you probably said, "Mary, what time is it?" Mary then proceeded to tell you the exact time. Although asking for the information and giving the information were parts of your conversation, they did not require a great deal of *interaction* by either of you. This simple process is comparable to the process you follow when you open up your history book and read in one of the chapters a listing of the Presidents of the United States. The only active parts of this process, on your part, are the opening of the book, the asking of the question, "Who are the Presidents of the United States?", and your use of your eyes to find the page where the names are listed.

Compare this to another conversation you might recently have had with a friend. This time you are discussing the values of going to college, and your friend says to you, "College is valuable only insofar as you get to know the right people so you can get a good job when you graduate." You reply that you disagree; you indicate that college also has value in helping you learn a great deal about the world that you did not know before. Your friend then begins to argue his point, giving you example after example of friends of his who did not learn anything new at college. After listening to this, you then proceed to give evidence for your position.

Let us stop here and analyze the process of your conversation. Note that this conversation is quite different from simply asking your friend for the time of day. You are now engaged in an active discussion of a par-

ticular question which may have more than one answer. Therefore, you listen carefully to your friend as he develops his argument and then proceed to give your own explanation for your point of view. This is an active conversation: there is a "give-and-take" between both people involved in the discussion. Good reading is similar to this involved and active process.

Good reading means, therefore, that you must "listen" to the author, evaluate his ideas, consider them in view of your own previously learned ideas, and then come to some conclusions about the worth of the author's ideas. Such a process implies that this kind of reading goes beyond reading for information and reading for pure enjoyment. It is the kind of reading which is necessary in college. To meet most course-demands, you will have to go beyond simply obtaining information and reading for enjoyment. It is this involved, active mental process that I shall discuss in the rest of this section.

If I divide this process into four major types of reading, you should be able to understand better what I am referring to. Let me list the four major types of reading here: they are *superficial, analytic, interpretive,* and *critical.* Let us look at each of these types of reading in more detail.

By *superficial reading,* I mean reading only for the obvious information which your reading matter contains or simply to obtain information. Your asking for the time of day is a good illustration. You are also reading superficially when you are interested only in the plot of a novel. You use this type of reading to look up information, for escape, or for pleasure reading. In superficial reading you are concerned primarily with the "who, what, when, and where" of the material; you are not concerned with long-time retention of the material or application of this reading to other material.

It should be clear now that superficial reading is usually *not* sufficient to meet most course-demands. This type of reading can be beneficial and useful only when you are interested in the superficial aspects of the material.

There are, of course, certain skills needed for this type of reading. For example, you must have a basic vocabulary that will make it possible for you to understand the words used in the selection. However, we can say that it is only an "acquaintanceship" vocabulary which is required. Another skill which is needed is the ability to connect one idea to another as you proceed in the reading. Since superficial reading is usually carried on with non-complicated writing, the connecting of one idea to another typically proceeds from one sentence to another. Another skill required for superficial reading is a minimum background of information related to the selection. You must have some already learned material that serves as a backdrop for this new information.

You should be able to see now that superficial reading is what we could call the minimum level of reading required in college work. *Analytic reading* follows, after you have the ability to handle superficial reading. Analytic reading is more complicated. Here you are interested in the comprehension of the main ideas, their relationships, and their derivation. In other words, you are interested in the total structure of the selection and the place of each part within the total structure. You are also concerned with the "why" as well as the "who, what, when, and where." In analytic reading you should also be concerned with understanding the material well enough to use it later or make some application of its ideas.

You can see that analytic reading goes far beyond superficial reading. Now you are concerned with more than simple facts; you are concerned with how these facts are put together to build ideas. You are interested in how the author established relationships among several ideas and how he derived his conclusion. Further, you want to be able to have complete recall of the material. Perhaps through rote learning, you will fix it in your memory, so that you can use it later.

To achieve this type of reading certain skills are also needed. These include an advanced vocabulary: by this I mean comprehension of the more subtle meanings of words and thus a better understanding and use of words than is necessary in superficial reading. As you know, many words have more than one meaning. For example, the word *sharp* can mean well-honed, as in "a sharp knife"; but it can also mean intelligent, as in "he is a sharp person"; or antagonistic, as in "that was a sharp remark." Understanding the differences in the meaning of such a word as *sharp* is necessary in analytic reading.

Connecting ideas logically is another ability needed. This means that you must be able to use the rules of logic to put together the various ideas presented by the author. This ability you can gain either by experience or by formally learning the rules of logic. A third ability required is that of being able to relate the ideas of a particular selection to ideas from other reading, courses, or lectures. A fourth requirement is the ability to remember the major and minor ideas. Once again we see that analytic reading goes beyond superficial in requiring that you remember the minor ideas as well as the major.

The two types of reading which I have just discussed—superficial and analytic—are required in most college courses. The two remaining types of reading are usually needed in more advanced courses. Take, for example, the third type of reading—interpretive. In *interpretive reading* you are interested in taking the ideas of a selection and determining their meaning for other ideas, events, or problems. You can see that interpretive reading is even more complicated than analytic reading. Here you are interested in more than the information presented in the selection. You are trying to go beyond the material presented and to extrapolate the ideas of the selection; you want to see the logical consequences of the ideas presented. To make this seem more concrete, let me give an example. If, in a conversation with a friend, you have discovered that his parents are against letting him use the family car, you can probably see the logical consequences of their position. It is not too difficult to predict that your friend will attempt either to borrow rides from his friends or to argue with his parents about the use of their car. In other words, you extrapolate or go beyond the known information by seeing the logical consequence of the parents' position.

As pointed out above, interpretive reading is required by some courses, usually at the advanced level. Here is where your knowledge of course-demands comes in. If you have discovered that a particular course requires you to go beyond the information presented in the required books and articles, you can see that your professor is requiring you to use interpretive reading. This is frequently true in English literature and philosophy courses and in certain advanced social science courses.

Let us see what skills are unique to this type of reading. You should keep in mind that all the skills required for analytic reading are also necessary here. You must have an advanced vocabulary, you must have the abilities to connect ideas logically, to relate ideas from this selection to ideas you have drawn from other reading, and to remember the major and minor ideas presented in the material. Beyond these skills there are particular ones necessary for interpretive reading. First, you must have the ability to abstract subtle meanings from the ideas presented; you must be able to see how certain ideas, when put together, give you an additional meaning that was not there before. Second, you must be able to see the logical consequences of a particular line of reasoning: you must be able to see that 32 follows 8, 16, 24.

Finally we come to the last type of reading, *critical reading*, which is the most complicated of all. In this type, you are interested in evaluating or judging the true quality of a selection. In other words, now you must go beyond the reading itself and, using certain standards, make a judgment about it. This type of reading is required by only a few courses at the undergraduate level in college. However, since you may be taking these courses, it is crucial that you understand the difference between critical and interpretive reading. Courses in the humanities, such as poetry, music, and art, are most likely to require this type of ability in the junior and senior years. Some of the social science courses, such as history, political science, or sociology, may also require this kind of reading ability.

Let us see what specific skills, in addition to those already required for analytic and interpretive reading, are needed in this type. The first is the ability to select and apply an appropriate criterion for judging the selection. This means that, as reader, you must be able to decide what standards are appropriate to apply to this particular reading. For example, in order to judge the quality of a football game, you use the rules of football, not the rules of baseball. So, with critical reading, you must select the appropriate criteria for judging that particular material.

The second is the ability to account for your own biases. By this I mean that you must be able to identify your own personal likes and dislikes and eliminate or take into account your subjective reactions, wherever possible, in making your critical analysis. To illustrate, if you have a bias against modern poetry, you must take it into account when you attempt to read critically a poem coming out of the present generation of poets. Thus, in critical reading, not only must you know your vocabulary, be able to connect ideas logically, relate the ideas in the selection to other materials, obtain subtle meanings from the ideas, and see the logical consequences from the material, but you must also apply non-biased criteria to the reading material.

In view of this discussion, you should now realize that reading as a self-demand has several facets. Because there are several types of reading and because there are various other abilities involved in reading (remembering, for example), you cannot say that you have *one* reading ability. As with the other self-demands, a thorough understanding of this self-demand requires knowledge of all aspects of your reading ability. You must be able to determine how well you can handle each of the four types of reading. Further, you must determine which types you prefer, since you may be able to read well analytically, for example, but prefer only superficial reading; or, by contrast, you may prefer to read critically but be able to read only superficially.

Relationship of Reading to Course-Demands

The relationship of reading to course-demands is also complex. Obviously, most college courses require you to read materials; however, there are wide differences in the types of reading required. As I mentioned above, some courses demand only superficial reading; others demand interpretive and critical reading. Therefore, you must be able to carry out the types of reading required if you are going to meet the course-demands. If your self-demands include a preference for, and ability to handle, analytical reading but your course-demands require critical reading, you will probably not succeed academically unless you are willing and can learn to read critically.

There is another way of viewing this complexity. Your self-demands may include a preference for analytical reading; you discover, however, that a particular course requires only superficial reading. You are now faced with this question: should you meet your self-demand for analytical reading or merely satisfy the simpler course-demand? If you do the former, it may make *you* feel better, but you will probably be wasting time and energy insofar as getting a high grade in the course is concerned. If you do the latter, you will be meeting the course-demand, but you will probably feel guilty because you will not be meeting your self-demand! Once again, you see that your behavior is influ-

enced by the type of success you desire (part of your self-demands) and by the goals of the college (part of the course-demands).

Speaking practically, then, if you want to meet the course-demands, you must figure out the types of reading required and determine if you can accomplish them. If you cannot, you must then develop those abilities. Stating it differently, you must modify your self-demand (reading ability).

Modifying Reading as a Self-Demand

I have already indicated the first step necessary for modifying this self-demand. You must determine the types of reading you can use well and the types you prefer. Second, you must spend considerable time, energy, and effort in practice so as to improve the types of reading you handle poorly. At the same time, you must understand why you prefer certain types of reading and discover the value of using other types. Third, you must practice using your newly-developed skills when you study. Fourth, you must reassess your reading abilities and preferences periodically to guarantee that the modifications become permanent.

Although these steps may seem rather simple, you should not assume that you can change your reading abilities and preferences without considerable effort and probably some pain. As we have already seen, by the time you reach college your reading has become habitual. Thus, change here involves changing habits. We have previously discussed the complexities of this type of self-demand.

Because of this, you will probably find that changing your reading abilities and preferences can best be accomplished with the help of experts. At most colleges today you will find special reading courses, laboratories, or clinics. These are frequently offered through the Dean of Students' Office or by the English department. Your college counselor can also help you, by discussing with you any reading tests you may have already taken.

In addition to utilizing these resources, you can also confer with your professors. They can help you determine the types of reading required; in addition, some instructors will be willing to work with you in helping you learn to read the material used in their courses.

Finally, you can work on your own to change this self-demand. There are a number of excellent books and manuals available that you can use for self-study. I have listed several of these references at the end of this chapter. You should keep in mind, however, that working on your own may not prove fruitful because of your other self-demands. Your habits, attitudes, personality needs, and unconscious factors may interfere. If this does occur, you should not be surprised, and you can then follow the other alternatives discussed above.

LISTENING

Nature of Listening

A simple way of describing listening is to say *it is the ability to pay attention to sounds and noises in the environment.* When you pay attention to these sounds and noises, you are conscious of their existence and thus have "listened" to them.

Although you have been listening to conversations, lectures, and discussions for many years, your ability to listen carefully probably "just grew" like Topsy. That is, in contrast to learning to read, it is likely that you have simply listened, without formally setting aside any time to learn to listen. Yet I think you will conclude, after analyzing the meaning of this word carefully, that listening is a distinct self-demand whose modification requires special attention.

Perhaps the simplest way to point this out is to show that various senses are involved in listening. You recall from the above section that reading involves the eyes and certain written symbols. Listening, of course, involves primarily the ears and certain sound symbols. Because you probably take for granted your ability to listen, you may ignore the various ways in which your ears can function.

Let me give you an example to illustrate the fact that listening can be carried on in different ways. Right now, if you have a radio or television set on, leave it on. If you do not, turn one on; now listen to the radio or TV for one minute, without attempting to read the rest of this section.

Now read this paragraph while attempting to shut out the sound of the radio or TV. If you are successful in doing this, you are proving to yourself that you can listen to certain sounds voluntarily. If you do not hear the sound of the radio or TV while you are reading these words, this shows that you are selecting the sounds in your environment to which you will pay attention. Thus, you are listening selectively.

Now that I have established the fact that you listen in a volnutary way, it is natural that we should turn to another point. What leads you to listen to some things and not to others? It is the various purposes or goals which motivate you which also select for you what you will listen to. As with reading, your purposes are to obtain information as a basis for new learning, to find enjoyment, or to solve problems. What you listen to, therefore, will depend upon your particular purpose at that particular time. In the above experiment, you were able to shut out the sounds of the radio or TV because you were not interested in using that source to obtain information for new learning, seek enjoyment, or solve problems. On the contrary, you were concentrating on the words written in this section. Because you were reading, you were unable to listen attentively at the same time.

The fact that you cannot listen carefully and concentrate on reading at the same time may be difficult for you to accept. Perhaps when you have been studying, you have had the radio or television on while reading. And yet I challenge you to prove that you were able to listen consciously while concentrating on your reading. This is not to say that you cannot *hear* background music or words while reading; *hearing* is quite different, however, from *listening* to the music or a speech.

Thus, we come to a discussion of the different types of listening which are possible. The categories that were established for reading apply here also. *Listening can be superficial, analytic, interpretive, or critical.* We have, in fact, already illustrated the first type. When you are listening to background music and are at the same time doing something else, such as studying, you are carrying on *superficial listening.* You also listen superficially when you are not concerned with the long-time retention or the application to other materials of what you hear. As with the first type of reading, certain skills are necessary. These include functioning ears, so that the sounds can be heard, a basic vocabulary, the ability to make simple connections between one idea and another, and a minimum background of information related to what is heard. In other words, superficial listening is really the type of listening which you carry on, day in and day out, in your social relations in the family and with friends.

Frequently, students assume that in courses which are predominantly of the lecture type only superficial listening is required, because they think their task is simply to listen to the words spoken and to take notes on this material. If your only purpose in attending a lecture is to transpose the information from the lecturer's notes to your own, then it is true that superficial listening is all that you need. As you will note below, however, listening of a different type is typically required in most college courses.

The second type of listening is *analytic.* Analytic listening, like analytic reading, goes beyond the superficial level. Here you are interested in the comprehension of the main ideas, their relationships, and their derivation. You try to find the total structure of what you are listening to and identify each of the parts in that structure. Further, you are concerned with the "why" as well as the

"who, what, when, and where" aspects of what you are listening to. You can see that analytic listening requires the same active process that is demanded by analytic reading. Whereas you can listen superficially while accomplishing other tasks, analytic listening requires your entire attention. If you are listening to your lectures analytically, you must be concentrating entirely upon the material presented by the teacher.

The same is true of *interpretive listening.* We have already spoken about the meaning of extrapolation. The same process is involved in interpretive listening. When you listen interpretively, you try to go beyond the material and see its logical consequences. I think you can see that both analytic and interpretive listening are typically required in class discussion or debates. The class discussion is usually centered on material that has been previously assigned; therefore, if you can go beyond the material presented and offer new ideas based upon that material, you will be able to show that you can listen to other members of the class or to the teacher in an analytic or interpretive manner. Once again, you should notice the active process involved. The class discussion is typically a constantly moving conversation about ideas. The fact that the discussion moves from point to point means that frequently the student must go beyond superficial listening.

The final type of listening—*critical listening*—is also extremely important for class discussions, debating, and similar activities. When I discussed critical reading above, I mentioned that it is different from other types of reading insofar as it requires that you select and apply appropriate criteria for judging and be able to account for your own biases. The same is true of critical listening. As I mentioned above, class discussions frequently require that you evaluate remarks by the teacher or other students. You must be able to use appropriate criteria or standards to judge the material presented while listening in class; likewise, as you listen to others present their ideas, you must be able to eliminate your own biases.

Looking at these four different types of listening, you can see that people can vary greatly in this self-demand. Some prefer and can achieve only superficial listening. Others may prefer critical but can achieve only analytical listening. Still others may have no preferences but can achieve all four types.

Relationship of Listening to Course-Demands

In the above section I have mentioned some of the relationships of listening to course-demands. The most obvious ones concern Activities. As you know, most college courses include lectures. Many also involve class participation or discussion. These Activities obviously require listening. Courses can vary widely, however, in the *types* of listening they require for these class activities. It would be a grave mistake to assume that all lectures require only superficial listening; likewise, it would be equally disastrous to assume that all class discussions require interpretive or critical listening.

Knowing that lectures and discussions are part of a course does not tell you what type of listening ability is required. You can know this only after you have determined the types of listening ability the professor demands. As we saw in Chapter V, this requires careful observation of the professor, of the tests and papers he gives, and of his evaluation procedures.

Modifying Listening as a Self-Demand

If you discover that your course-demands require types of listening which you do not prefer or cannot achieve, you must change this self-demand if you desire academic success. But how can you do this? Fortunately, except for certain genetic problems that I shall mention shortly, you can use the same methods I discussed for changing your reading abilities. These include: (1) determining the types of listening you can do well and the types you prefer; (2) practicing to improve

the types you use poorly; (3) practicing the newly-developed skills in and out of classes; and (4) reassessing your listening abilities and preferences periodically to guarantee that the modifications become permanent.

Accomplishing the first step in this process is not as easy as it is for reading, because you will not have access to standardized listening tests that can point out your ability to accomplish the four types of listening. The tests that are available can, however, help you identify any malfunctioning of your ears. In this way you can determine whether there are any genetic reasons for poor listening ability. Most college health services (or speech and hearing clinics) carry out such tests. By utilizing this service, you can determine whether you possess the necessary physical components for modifying your listening ability.

Assuming that you do, you are still faced with the problem of estimating your ability to handle the four types of listening. There are several informal procedures you can follow. One is to compare what you and your fellow students obtain from lectures. Pick out several classmates who seem to understand well the lectures you all attend, and then estimate your superficial listening ability by discussing the "who, what, when, and where" aspects of a lecture with them. If your friends seem to be able to recall much more of these factual elements than you do, you can conclude that you probably do not listen as well as they. (As we shall see later, however, the kind of notes you take during the lecture can influence how well you recall its content.)

You can make the same kind of estimate by listening to a radio program with these friends. If they are able to recall much more of the program's content than you, you can once again conclude that your superficial listening ability is probably in need of improvement.

Estimating your level of analytic, interpretive, and critical listening abilities can probably best be determined by comparing your understanding of an involved class discussion with that of your classmates. You can estimate this by noting how well you follow the discussion. Are you able to see the relationships of the ideas presented? Are you able to see the logical consequences of the arguments of the speakers? Are you able to determine the criteria they are using for making their judgments?

If you are not able to answer these questions, you can use two sources to help you. You can ask a classmate to give you his estimate, or you can ask your professor to indicate how he evaluates you in comparison with the other class members. In each case, you must explain clearly the types of judgment you desire.

From the above, you should notice that estimating your level of these abilities requires you either to write (notes) or to speak of what you have heard. In other words, you cannot get an estimate of your listening abilities without also displaying to some extent your abilities to write or speak. This illustrates a point that we shall see time and time again: *the separate self-demands are so interwoven that a modification of one is likely to influence the others.* In this case, improving your writing and speaking abilities will probably help your listening abilities.

Modifying your listening abilities can proceed once you have made the above-mentioned estimates. As you might expect, it should be easier to modify your superficial listening ability than the other three. Since this requires simply recalling the "who, what, when, and where"—the content—the main task is to make yourself concentrate on what you are hearing. As you recall from our discussion, you control (consciously or unconsciously) what you listen to. In other words, if you catch yourself *not* listening to a lecture or class discussion, you have closed your mind to registering the sounds your ears have picked up. Your main task, then, is to discover why your mind has consciously or unconsciously closed itself to these sounds. Here is where your knowledge of your other

self-demands can be helpful. If you understand many of your personality needs and attitudes, you may discover that the content of the lecture is repugnant to you, or you may discover that the lecturer causes you to react negatively. Your negative reactions can unconsciously lead you to close your mind to the sounds you hear.

The same results may occur because of other self-demands. If your goals and reasons for going to college are inconsistent with those of the class lecture or discussion, you will not have any real interest in the course content. As a result, your mind (usually unconsciously) turns to other topics that are more related to your goals.

Thus, *lack of superficial listening ability probably can be best corrected by modifying the other self-demands that are interfering with this ability.* Putting it another way, if your goals and reasons are similar to the course's, and your personality needs and attitudes fit the course, your superficial listening ability should be at a high level.

The one exception to this occurs when your writing or speaking abilities interfere. For example, if your note-taking is so slow or so demanding that you can concentrate only on this process, obviously you will not be able to listen to the lecture. You will hear it but not remember it, since your mind is preoccupied. You may be very interested and highly motivated to learn the course content, but your low writing ability interferes. I shall have more to say about this when we look at writing as a self-demand.

While your superficial listening ability can be greatly modified by changing your other self-demands, analytic, interpretive, and critical listening also require considerable practice in listening. These abilities require more than concentration; because they require, in addition to concentration, the ability to figure out relationships, to extrapolate ideas, or to apply suitable criteria, you must practice the latter aspects. Probably the best way of practicing is to work with the instructor of the course. If he is willing to work with you after a class is over, for example, you can compare the relationships you have identified with the ones he identified. If he is not available, you can do the same thing with another classmate. In this case, you may be able to practice over the period of an entire semester.

Another possible way of changing this self-demand is to take certain college courses that tend to emphasize the more difficult listening abilities. Usually speech, literature, and philosophy courses include this course-demand. In this manner you will be forced to practice, since the professors of these courses usually spend time in teaching or illustrating these abilities.

Another possible way of improving is to practice listening to radio or television programs while at the same time recording these sessions on tape. First, make notations of what you hear as well as your reactions to this information, and then check this over while you replay the taped talks or discussions. In this manner, you will have a permanent record which you can use time and again for self-criticism. Such a technique might also be used in a classroom. Assuming that you obtain permission from the instructor, you can tape a class lecture or discussion which you can then play back later, comparing the way in which you heard the ideas presented earlier with your present impressions.

Finally, I have listed at the end of the chapter a number of fine books and articles which will give you specific hints about improving your listening abilities. I think you will find that practicing the suggested ideas and rules will increase your achievement in this area.

QUESTIONING

Questioning and Course-Demands

I would guess that most students do not think of questioning as a necessary ability involved in obtaining academic success. And yet, as we shall see, this is a very important self-demand. Unfortunately, as with listening, most of us are unaware of our questioning ability. Further, you probably have not even considered whether you can improve this ability. Therefore, let me explain the nature of questioning and point out how it is related to other self-demands and course-demands.

Questioning means that we do not accept everything as given. Or, stating it another way, it means to ask questions about something, either silently or out loud. As with reading and listening, you can list a number of different purposes for using questioning. For example, questioning can be used to obtain information, to challenge the accuracy or completeness of an idea or thing, to challenge the value of an idea or thing, to satisfy an intrinsic curiosity, or to serve as an aid in reading or listening. Let us look at each of these purposes separately. It should be obvious to you that questions are used to obtain information. Earlier we used the example of your asking a friend for the time of day. The purpose of this question was to obtain information. This is, of course, the purpose most frequently achieved by asking questions. However, in college other purposes can be even more valuable. Take the second one listed above: to challenge the accuracy or completeness of an idea or thing. In those courses that involve more than information-giving, you may be required to check the accuracy or completeness of a book, of a research report, or perhaps of some information the teacher has given the class. Raising the appropriate question will help you find out the degree of accuracy or completeness of your source.

The third purpose of questioning that I have listed—to challenge the value of an idea or thing—is probably most useful in those courses which present general points of view rather than specific facts. For example, philosophy, literature, and other courses in the humanities as well as advanced courses in the social sciences, are most likely to require this kind of questioning. When you compare and contrast different poems, pieces of music, or philosophical systems, you are, in a sense, challenging the value of these things. To accomplish this, you must be able to raise intelligent questions.

Children, especially, use questions for the fourth purpose. If you observe a young child, you will note that he raises questions simply out of what we call intrinsic curiosity. It is a child's intrinsic curiosity which prompts him to ask questions when he has no motivation but to discover the why or wherefore of a particular thing. Unfortunately, as we got older and more sophisticated, many of us learned to curb this intrinsic curiosity. As adults we frequently feel that there is a social pressure which prevents us from innocently raising questions which may, at the same time, prove embarrassing. As a college student, however, you should certainly attempt to satisfy your curiosity by raising questions.

The final reason why college students raise questions is that questioning is an aid in reading or listening. In our earlier discussion of the skills involved and steps required in different types of reading and listening, I mentioned that questions must be raised along the way. For example, in interpretive and critical reading and listening, you must ask yourself about the particular logical consequences of the ideas, as well as the appropriate standards which you should use in criticizing a particular piece. In this way questioning has a distinctive value in helping you read and listen.

Questioning, like reading and listening, involves several distinct elements. First, you must have a minimum level of information if you are to raise questions at all. Have you had the experience of being exposed to a new course in an area for which you have had no previous background? Perhaps in the first day or so of this new exposure, you have felt completely lost and without any guidelines. Probably during this time you did not have that minimum level of information referred to above, but once you do have a bare minimum of information, it is possible to begin to raise questions. The second necessary ele-

ment in questioning is the ability to identify important points that need questioning. If, as a student, you confuse the major and minor points of a lecture, it makes it almost impossible to raise the appropriate questions. The skill necessary to identify the important points comes out of a previously developed ability in listening. Raising questions which are capable of meaningful solution is the last necessary element in good questioning. It is possible for you to have a minimum level of information and to be able to identify important points that need questioning but still lack skill in posing questions. However, this type of skill comes mainly with practice; thus, if you do not raise questions, the chances of developing this skill are very slim. I shall discuss below ways in which the phrasing of questions can be improved.

By now you probably realize that questioning is required by several course-demands. It is especially important in preparing for class work, participating in class discussions, and taking quizzes and examinations. When you use interpretive and critical reading to handle the assigned references, you will need to be able to ask questions. Through the questioning process, you can prepare for class work in a more thorough manner. We will discuss this further when we look at the ability to remember.

We discussed above the problem of concentration and superficial listening. At that time I pointed out that problems in concentration frequently result from differences in goals that lead to a lack of motivation. Now you can see that questioning can be used as an artificial means of increasing your ability in superficial listening. When poor concentration is a problem, posing questions can force you to concern yourself with the material. In other words, you create for yourself specific goals that are more closely related to the course-demands. Thus, raising questions before, during, and after reading a selection can help screen out other sounds and thoughts and thus help you to concentrate, just as asking questions while you are listening will help you to focus on what you hear. This is an important reason why modifying this self-demand can help you to obtain academic success.

Modifying Questioning as a Self-Demand

Modifying this self-demand, however, can be thwarted if you are unaware of your attitude toward using this ability. Whereas you probably have a positive attitude toward doing the reading and listening required to meet course-demands, you may have a negative attitude toward asking questions, either while you are doing your assignments or when you are participating in class. In other words, you may have the ability to question but, because of your negative attitude, fail to use it.

Because this attitude is so prevalent, I want to dwell a bit more on this point. Why might you feel negative toward raising questions? If you recall my discussion of attitudes in Chapter VIII, you will remember that negative attitudes evolve because you have come to associate pain with the particular object, person, or condition which evokes this reaction, or because you have copied another person who has displayed such an attitude. Thus, we can guess that if you have a negative attitude toward questioning it may have come about because you experienced pain when you raised questions before. Perhaps you have earlier been embarrassed by the reactions of other students or the teacher to your questions: if you asked "foolish" questions, you were probably ridiculed or laughed at. Since you have learned, over time, that raising questions only produces frustration, your negative attitude has developed.

You may also have developed a negative attitude toward questioning through your identification with another person. Because most adolescents tend to identify with one or more older adolescents, if the latter "pooh-pooh" raising questions in class or in studying, the former do likewise. Since older adolescents tend to view questioning as "apple-polishing," someone whom you admired may have discredited questioning, and you have, thus, tended to do so too. As I have pointed out above, however, questioning is a very important ability required by many college courses. Thus, you must modify your negative attitude if you are to succeed. Assuming that you are able to do this by following the steps outlined in Chapter VIII, your next task is to determine your present level of this ability.

Unfortunately, as with listening, there are no standardized tests to help you identify how well you can raise questions. Accordingly, you will have to rely on informal procedures. One such technique is self-observation. If you compare the way you raise questions in classes with your classmates' abilities, it should be relatively easy to estimate your ability compared to theirs. You should notice the number and the kinds of questions that are raised. This should indicate whether you tend to ask informational, evaluative, or critical questions.

In addition, you can obtain an estimate of your ability by asking your professor to evaluate your questions. He can compare you with many students. Further, he can indicate if the questions you ask are the kinds of questions you should be raising in his class. Your classmates can also aid in this procedure, since they probably view your questioning differently from the professor.

These sources of information should indicate the aspects of questioning that need to be modified. Several methods can be used at this point. One is to study the questions raised in your classes by your professors. By studying the phrasing of a teacher's questions in relation to the course-demands, you should be able to derive a model for the kind of questioning suitable to that particular course and decide what type of questions are necessary in it. Another way in which you can improve your questioning skills is by studying the questions presented in your books. Most textbooks have a series of questions at the end of each chapter. If you will note how these questions are constructed, the parts of the chapters from which they come, and the type of questions raised, you have another source of information. You can take a different book and practice creating questions of the same sort as those which you have noted in other books. You can then ask your instructor to check them for their value in studying. You can also improve your questioning skills in another way: after learning thoroughly some of the material for a course, you can then try to develop questions on this information. You can estimate the worth of these questions by asking another person to answer them and watching his reactions. He should be able to tell you the degree of help which these questions provide.

A note of caution must be made at this point. You may already have the habit of raising a number of questions in class, and, therefore, you may assume that you already know the various ways in which questions can be used. You should bear in mind, however, that it is possible to use questioning to satisfy particular personality needs. You can use questioning as a way to challenge authority: by asking numerous, and perhaps difficult, questions of the instructor, you may have a feeling of triumph over authority. I am sure you can see that this is carried on in an unconscious way, but it can, nevertheless, interfere with learning in the classroom. Although it is difficult for you to make an analysis of your own involvement in questioning, perhaps the simple guideline which I am suggesting here will be helpful. If you

find yourself repeatedly asking many questions which give you a certain inner satisfaction other than the satisfaction of obtaining information or carrying out other types of learning, this is probably a sign that you are using questioning to satisfy an unconscious personality need. If this is the case, perhaps a discussion with your college counselor would be helpful here.

You can also improve your questioning ability by following the ideas presented in several other books. I have listed some of the available sources at the end of this chapter. Whether you follow those suggestions or the ones listed above, you should realize that considerable practice is necessary to change this self-demand. However, from this practice you should receive the pleasure that can lead to the development of valuable questioning habits.

CHAPTER SUMMARY

There are several reasons why abilities can usually be modified. Probably foremost is the fact that you can logically determine your weakness and practice the desired change. In this chapter we have looked at the ways reading, listening, and questioning can be improved. I have explained each in some detail, pointed out its relationship to course-demands, and described specific means of modifying it. Since you have carried on reading, listening, and questioning for many years, maintaining these changes will require considerable practice.

THOUGHT QUESTIONS

1. What kind of reading is most difficult for you? Why? What could you do to change this situation?
2. What kinds of reading are most frequently required by your course-demands? What meaning does this have for you?
3. Do your courses require interpretive or critical listening? How do you know this? What implication does this have for modifying your listening ability?

4. What kind of attitude toward questioning do you have? Why? How does this attitude influence your questioning ability?
5. How can listening and questioning abilities be used to improve your reading ability? Why would this occur?

SELECTED REFERENCES

Modifying Reading

Flesch, Rudolf, and others. *How You Can Be a Better Student.* New York: Sterling, 1957. Chapter 4.

Lass, Abraham H. *How to Prepare for College.* New York: David White, 1962. Chapters 5–6.

Morgan, Clifford T., and Deese, James. *How to Study.* New York: McGraw-Hill, 1957. Chapters 3, 4.

Witty, Paul. *Streamline Your Reading.* Chicago: Science Research Associates, 1960. Chapters 1–7.

Modifying Listening

Farquhar, William W., and others. *Learning to Study.* New York: Ronald Press, 1960. Chapter 7.

Floyd, Mary F. *Let's Talk,* rev. ed. Chicago: Science Research Associates, 1960. Chapter 7.

Robinson, Frances P. *Effective Study,* rev. ed. New York: Harper, 1961. Chapter 7.

Modifying Questioning

Centi, P., and Doyle, P. A. *Basic College Skills.* New York: Rinehart, 1959.

Dudycha, George J. *Learn More with Less Effort.* New York: Harper, 1957. Chapter 5.

Morgan, Clifford T., and Deese, James. *How to Study.* New York: McGraw-Hill, 1957. Chapters 3, 6.

CHAPTER XI

Abilities: Remembering, Writing, and Speaking

We shall now look at three other abilities that are usually modifiable. As you read this chapter, compare this discussion with the ideas presented in Chapter X. You should see considerable interdependence in the ways in which all of these abilities can be modified.

REMEMBERING

The Nature of Remembering

All of your life you have had to remember different things, but you have probably never stopped to ask yourself, "What is remembering?" *By remembering I mean the ability to recognize or recall something for a certain period of time.* This time period may be of long or short duration. By recognition I mean that you are aware of the meaning of certain symbols. For example, when you read the word "football," you note that it refers to a leather ball that is used in the game of football. In other words, you are given the word-symbol, football, and you recognize its meaning. When you remember through the process of recall, however, you are not given any symbol. An idea or a piece of information must come from your own mind, your memory. For example, if I ask you, "When did Columbus discover America?" and, after "searching" your mind for this fact which you learned a long time ago, you answer, "1492," you have indicated recall.

Both recognition and recall can result from either deliberate or unconscious processes on your part. I am sure that you have deliberately tried to remember certain pieces of information throughout your formal education. You may have done this by repeating a specific fact a number of times, until, after a while, you were able to recall this fact when you needed it. For example, this is probably how you would learn the name of a chemical equation you want to remember. On the other hand, there are many things that you remember without recalling how you learned them; in this case, you have stored the fact in your memory through an unconscious process. To illustrate, you may be able to recall clearly a particular event that occurred earlier in your life, although it may be difficult for you to remember how you learned it or had it imprinted on your memory.

Both the deliberate and unconscious aspects of remembering are influenced by your motivation and perception. You will learn things deliberately at times because you are highly motivated by your desire to have this material in your memory. The motivation can be of an intrinsic or extrinsic nature. For example, if the last time that you memorized a list of words you did so in order to get a reward (a grade) that was not in itself part of the process of memorization, you were acting under extrinsic motivation. On the other hand, you can remember other things unconsciously because of another kind of motivation. Intrinsic motivation—doing something because there is pleasure in the process of doing it—is not only an unconscious process, however; you can deliberately rely on it as well. Learning a poem for the sheer joy of remembering it is an example of this. How you perceive—that is how your senses react to a particular piece of information or condition—also influences what you remember. Since perceptions are also influenced by

motivation, it should be easy for you to see the connection between how well you remember things and how you see them.

Because you probably equate the term "remembering" with "memory," I would suggest that remembering may be the more useful term, since it refers to the different *kinds* of remembering as well as the things that you remember; however, both memory and remembering are essentially the same thing.

Relationship of Remembering to Course-Demands

As you might guess, there is a very close relationship between remembering and various course-demands. To explain this statement, I shall discuss the various types of things you can remember and how they are associated with course Activities and Regulations. You can remember intellectual, emotional, or physical things in your life. In the intellectual area, you can remember specific facts, such as names, dates, events, equations, patterns, and symbols; also, you can remember principles, processes, and attitudes. In the emotional area, you remember positive emotions, such as love, joy, glee, and the like, as well as negative emotions including hate, anger, and fear. Third, you can remember things in the physical realm, including motor skills, such as walking and jumping, and sensory experiences related to cold, heat, fatigue, and the like.

As you recall, remembering in reference to college work centers primarily on the intellectual. However, both emotional and physical memories have some significance too. As I noted earlier, your success in college is influenced by your personality and, therefore, the emotional patterns of your personality become involved in your efforts to succeed. As you know, if a negative emotion, such as anger toward teachers, is remembered well, the ability to learn in a particular teacher's class may be negatively influenced by the memory of this emotion. My point here is that although you do not consciously and deliberately try to remember emotional experiences, memories of them do exist and, therefore, may influence your efforts to succeed.

The physical things that you remember —motor skills and sensory experiences—are, likewise, not usually as crucial as the intellectual; however, they are important in some classes such as physical education, science laboratories, art, and music. Although you take for granted the memory of certain motor skills by the time you are of college age, for particular students the lack of memory of one of these skills may become crucial in one or two courses. If this is true in your case, this is something you must deal with adequately, just as you need to deal with memory in other areas.

Remembering in the intellectual area is probably the most crucial ability that you need while attending college. Almost all of the other abilities discussed in this book are either preparation for this ability or depend upon it. Most methods of evaluation or grading used by your professors are based upon your ability to remember the various intellectual things you have studied. Thus, tests in class as well as papers written outside of class require a great deal of recall or recognition. The fact that reading, listening, and questioning are important cannot be denied. And yet these three abilities have remembering as one of their major components and goals. Likewise, remembering is necessary before you can carry on reading, listening, or questioning. We will see that this is also true for all of the other abilities discussed later. In other words, not only is remembering crucial for meeting the course-demands, but it is also important for your other self-demands.

Modifying Remembering as a Self-Demand

The fact that remembering is so significant gives particular importance to the ways in which you can modify your ability to remember. Fortunately, there are several objective and subjective methods for determining the level of your ability. As part of some group and individual intelligence tests, a test of remembering is included. By analyzing existing test results, or arranging for such a test, you can obtain an estimate of your ability in comparison with a large number of other students and adults. Your college counselor is probably the best person to see about getting this information.

In addition to this procedure, you can also use your past experiences as a way of judging this ability. By the time you have reached college, you have taken many course examinations. Since most of these required either recall or recognition, your exam results should indicate how well you *have* remembered in the past. Since factors other than the ability to remember are usually involved in taking an exam, however, you should not view these results as a total indication of your potential ability. Nevertheless, these grades do show how you have typically been able to remember under examination conditions.

In addition to these two basic methods, you can estimate your ability through other techniques of observation. As I indicated in Chapters IV and VI, analyzing Non-School Activities and the reactions of Significant Others can be helpful. Such data can indicate how well you remember things outside of the formal educational setting and, thus, can give a different perspective to your analysis of your level of ability.

Once you have determined how well you can remember, you must then discover the techniques you now use for remembering. In this way you can determine if you should try to use additional methods to increase the level of your ability to remember. To do this, however, you must understand the various methods you use. Therefore, let me remind you of how you can make this analysis.

In Chapters IV, V, and VI, I discussed the types of learning that you can carry out. I indicated that you learn through trial and error, rote, association, conscious problem-solving, and unconscious insight. I also indicated that, by using one or more of these methods, learning occurs. In other words, the evidence that learning has occurred is that you have changed your behavior. Since these changes typically include remembering, you can say that when learning occurs, remembering has typically occurred. However, you should realize that some kinds of learning involve *much more* than remembering. They may require integration, comparison, and creation. Thus, although the types of learning you use are also the methods you use for remembering, *learning and remembering are not the same thing*. Remembering is simply one way in which you have evidence that learning has occurred. Integrating or creating are other ways of showing that other kinds of learning have taken place. I shall explain this point more fully in the following chapter.

Improving your ability to remember, then, is dependent on knowing which of these types of learning you use. After they have been identified, you can make an effort to add new methods or to improve on the ones you are already using. If you discover that you rely almost entirely upon rote, you might try to improve your remembering ability by adding, for example, association and conscious problem-solving methods. You saw earlier that using all of the methods is usually the best means for maximizing learning, and you can now see that the same is true for remembering.

If you are trying to remember some factual material, your ability will be highest if you use rote (say the facts over and over again), association (relate this new information to other facts you already remember), conscious problem-solving (try to answer questions about the new information), and unconscious insight (allow some time to pass if you get stuck in answering some questions).

This example should help you realize that most people can increase their ability to remember. However, because individuals vary widely in their inherited brain structure, some can increase their ability to a much larger extent than others. Here is a case where biological inheritance can limit your efforts to modify this self-demand.

Assuming that you are not extremely limited biologically, the next step in increasing your remembering ability is to do lots of practicing. If you want to add conscious problem-solving, you must practice carrying out this method. Since I shall go over specific ways of practicing this when I discuss modifying the types of learning later, in Chapter XIII, you can turn to that section if you want to study these methods now.

One last comment on changing your ability to remember. There are available several good, practical books on increasing this ability. The ones by Morgan and Deese and Voeks listed at the end of this chapter should prove especially helpful.

WRITING

The Nature of Writing

Simply stated, *writing is a way of expressing on paper ideas, feelings, attitudes, and so on, through language*. Although we can also write on other media, such as stone, wood, or glass, in our culture the use of paper is fairly standard. Generally we think of writing in a *word* language but, of course, we can also write in a *numerical* language. Arithmetic illustrates this. As we shall see later, writing is similar to speaking, except for the media involved and the use of different senses and symbols.

Writing in a word (verbal) language involves several elements: there must be motor coordination, the existence of a vocabulary, the ability to use certain rules of expression (grammar), and some ideas, feelings, or attitudes to be expressed.

Writing is a natural associate of reading, listening, questioning, and remembering. You normally write ideas down while, or after, performing these other abilities. In fact, writing down these ideas typically increases your level of achievement in the other abilities. I shall refer to this again shortly.

Before looking at the various types of writing, let us look at the different reasons for writing. The most elementary is to provide a record for future use. Man has used writing in this way ever since the dawn of recorded history. The desire to record ideas by writing them down is so basic that we often overlook its importance. Almost equally significant is the second reason for writing: to communicate to someone else ideas, feelings, and attitudes. Other than in the formal educational setting, you will use writing primarily for the second purpose. Letter-writing illustrates this well. Only a small proportion of people use writing for the third reason: for them, however, writing is a way of getting direct pleasure from the process of expressing ideas, feelings, or attitudes. Poets and novelists probably best illustrate those who write for the pleasure of writing itself.

In contrast, you may use writing for a fourth reason that is not directly related to gaining pleasure from the process of writing. You can use it as an aid in remembering. I mentioned above that writing can be used to increase the level of achievement of other abilities; this is particularly true for remembering. Let's see why this is so. You now know that you learn to remember by using trial and error, rote, association, conscious problem-solving, and unconscious insight. You also know that, in addition to intellectual things, you remember emotional and physical things. By connecting these two concepts, you can see why writing can aid remembering. If you use rote to remember some information, you repeat it over and over again. After a while, you have recall of this intellectual material. However, if you also write down the material, as you say it over and over again, you will then be developing recall of a physical thing. In other words, the physical movement of writing involves a physical sense organ—the touch sense in the fingers, hand, and arm—that also leads to remembering. In this case, what you will remember is a physical act as well as a mental one. Thus, you learn to remember two things simultaneously. When you try to recall the intellectual information, you automatically also recall the physical sensation. The two, working to-

gether, tend to strengthen your ability to remember the information.

In addition to this, writing aids remembering because the act of writing usually requires greater concentration than simply thinking of the information. Stating it another way, trying to write the information down creates a specific goal that tends to blot out other goals that might exist. As a result you are able to stick with an uninteresting task.

The same benefit occurs for questioning and listening. Writing down questions focuses your attention on the material and therefore helps you concentrate. The same process occurs when you take notes during a lecture. In addition, of course, taking notes gives you a record of the material for future use. I shall refer to this again later when I discuss writing and course-demands.

We can also look at the nature of writing from another angle. Let's view the various ways of classifying writing: these include *formal-informal, complete-partial,* and *finished-initial.* Formal writing refers to the style used in school, business, and industry, as well as the styles used in literature; it is the "approved" way of writing. Informal refers to the style you use in writing letters to friends or writing notes to relatives; it is writing in your "everyday" language. Complete means that the ideas are presented in sentences and paragraphs; whole ideas are included. Partial means that ideas are represented by words or phrases: note-taking is an example of this. Finished means that the writing is in final form, while initial means that the ideas are presented only in a first draft or rough form.

Classifying writing in these ways should help you realize that there is actually not *one* writing ability but many. In fact, as with reading, you may have high ability in some types but low ability in others. To make this point clearer, I shall now discuss the various kinds of formal writing that you can use. These include *descriptive, analytical, interpretive, critical-persuasive,* and *creative.*

Descriptive writing is writing in which you literally describe or tell about a fact, idea, feeling, or attitude. We see this type of writing about us all the time; most newspaper articles are of this nature. *Analytical writing* goes beyond mere description; it attempts to take its subject apart and identify its parts, so that the reasons for its existence are depicted. If you are writing an analysis of a car accident, you not only tell what happened but show why it happened. You "take apart" the whole accident and relate each part to the whole. Thus, you explain how the first driver failed to give a turn signal; as a result of this, the driver behind him did not have enough warning to avoid the accident; you will then point out that he also did not have enough time because he was driving too close to the first car.

In *interpretive writing* you go beyond descriptive and analytical writing because you try to make some inferences or draw some conclusions in addition to making an analysis. In the last example, you might indicate that the accident was the fault of the second driver. You are able to make this interpretation only if you know the driving regulations, which say that, regardless of other factors, a car following too closely behind another car is at fault if it rams into the first car. In this kind of writing, you attempt to go beyond the obvious data and give the reader your interpretation of the material you are writing about. You will see many examples of this kind of writing in magazine articles; newspaper columnists usually write in this style also.

When you use *critical-persuasive* writing you attempt to do two things: to make judgments about your subject and to try to convince others of your opinions. You must be able to analyze your material, apply some criteria for making judgments, and then write in a manner which will persuade your readers. You can persuade by appealing to the reader's reason, emotions, or both. Perhaps the most common examples of this type of writing are political speeches. In addition, we have examples in the advertising of all kinds of products, of industries, and of colleges. Propaganda, of course, heavily stresses the persuasive aspects of this kind of writing.

Although *creative writing* may involve critical-persuasive writing, it need not. The distinguishing characteristic of creative writing is originality. Your main goal in creative writing is to present some idea, feeling, or attitude in a new and unique way that may or may not describe it, analyze it, judge it, or convince others regarding it. You try to create, in your writing, a new way of viewing something; you try to express it so that the reader can also view it as you have done. Or, perhaps, you are not even concerned about the reader. You may write creatively simply because you obtain satisfaction from the process of writing; then creating something through writing is in itself enough reward. We refer to creative writers as poets, novelists, playwrights, and essayists.

Relationship of Writing to Course-Demands

There are various reasons for using writing and various types of writing. Before you attempt to modify your writing ability you must be able to relate your course-demands to this self-demand. Let me review with you some of the obvious relationships and point out some of the subtle ones.

Certainly for most courses writing is involved in many Regulations and Activities. Papers and reports are usually required. Taking quizzes and examinations also involve some type of writing. In addition, writing may also be necessary because of the Professor's Personality. He may subtly indicate that note-taking in class is expected, or his goals may also require note-taking if he demands exact recall of lecture material. This expectation may become clear only when you have seen the type of exams that he gives!

Further, the course's Goals may require certain types of writing. English literature, history, and philosophy, for example, may require critical-persuasive or creative writing;

psychology and biology may require only descriptive writing. Likewise, some courses may demand formal, complete, and finished writing, while others require only informal, partial, and initial writing. Success in these courses, therefore, can depend on how well you understand which of the various types of writing are required. It is only then that you know if you need to modify your writing abilities.

Modifying Writing as a Self-Demand

As with the other abilities, the first step in modifying your writing is to determine the level of your ability. Because there are various types, you must find out the level for each type. Most people, of course, vary from one to the other, although some have high abilities in all. Fortunately, there are some good ways of estimating these abilities. One method is to use standardized writing tests. You have probably already taken one or more of these during your high school years. Results of these may be available to you through your college counselor. If not, or in addition, you can arrange with him to take some. Several may be needed since they probably measure different aspects of writing ability.

In addition to test data, you can use your past high school and college course work as a guide. As I indicated in Chapters IV and VI, you can think over the kinds of writing you have done well and the kinds that have been difficult for you. Further, you can speak to your college professors to obtain their views of your writing abilities. You can also compare the way you take notes or write themes and reports with those of your friends. Regardless of the sources of your information, however, you should attempt to determine which of your writing abilities are the strongest and which are the weakest.

With this information available, you are now ready to modify this self-demand. Assuming that you need to modify one or more aspects of your writing, there are several procedures you can follow. One is participating in a writing clinic. Many colleges today, in addition to reading clinics, sponsor writing clinics or laboratories. Special personnel are hired to help students with writing problems. Another method is to sign up for courses that require certain kinds of writing abilities. This demands considerable courage on your part, since you know ahead of time that you will probably not get a good grade. However, it is in just such a course that the professor will usually take the time to help you with your writing difficulties. Typically, courses in English literature, creative writing, and journalism include such goals.

In addition to these more formal methods, there are two or three other ways you can modify your writing. If you know a friend who writes well, you can ask him to tutor you. You can also, on some campuses, locate advanced English majors who are willing to tutor for moderate fees. Finally, you can work on your own. There are some excellent, practical books available. Several of these are listed at the end of this chapter. The one by Flesch is especially good for developing note-taking. The one by Ruchlis is very good for formal styles of writing.

Two last comments about modifying this self-demand. Because your present writing abilities have evolved over a long period of time, you probably write in a habitual manner. Therefore, as we saw with modifying other abilities, modifying your writing may take considerable time and energy. Furthermore, because critical-persuasive and creative writing require highly-developed abstract thinking, your biological inheritance may limit the amount of modification you can achieve. However, you cannot determine this until you have tried to change the current levels of your writing ability.

SPEAKING

The Nature of Speaking

Although you may not think so, speaking is very similar to writing. As I discuss the ability to speak, I shall point out the many common characteristics. I shall also indicate the few crucial differences, so that you can see why your levels of ability to do each may vary greatly.

By looking at the nature of speaking you should be able to see the great similarity to writing. You can view *speaking as a way of expressing orally ideas, feelings, attitudes, and so on, through language.* This definition is exactly the same as for writing with one exception: instead of expressing the content on paper, you express yourself orally. Speaking involves primarily sound symbols; writing involves primarily visual symbols.

The elements necessary for speaking are very similar to those necessary for writing: these include motor coordination, the existence of an adequate vocabulary, the use of certain rules governing expression (grammar), and some ideas, feelings, or attitudes to be expressed. The main difference between speaking and writing rests in the types of motor coordination required. Writing involves eye, arm, hand, and finger movements; speaking, in contrast, involves tongue, mouth, larynx, throat, and chest movements.

Several other differences should be noted. One is that different types of remembering are involved. Writing requires recall of visual symbols; speaking demands recall of sound symbols. Also, the use of certain rules of expression are typically more demanding in writing than they are in speaking. Another difference is that a writing vocabulary requires accurate spelling, while spelling is not involved in a speaking vocabulary. Speaking, however, demands more self-assurance and poise; it is usually more difficult to speak to an audience (even of one) than to put your ideas on paper privately.

Despite these differences, you will use speaking for most of the same reasons you use writing. The main one is to communicate to someone else your ideas, feelings, and attitudes. Although formerly you would not have been able to use speech as a way of keeping a record of information, recent technological advances have now made it possible to do this; you can now use electrical disc and tape-recording methods to store oral information. You can also use speaking as a way of getting direct pleasure from the process of expressing yourself. In contrast to writing, which only a few people use for this reason, many people find speaking itself directly satisfying. Professionally, we see this evident in the actor.

Finally, as with writing, you can use speaking as an aid to remembering. It helps for essentially the same reasons that writing helps. As you attempt to remember by using rote, for example, you can say the material out loud. In this way, you learn to recall the visual symbols and, at the same time, learn the sound symbols. Because two senses become involved, greater remembering results. Further, because you have added a specific goal (trying to say the material as you think it), your concentration is aided. Thus, your mind stays with the task at hand. Practically speaking, this is why many students say to themselves or to others the information they want to remember.

So far I have pointed out that writing and speaking have many similarities in their functions. The same can be said of our ways of classifying them, as *formal-informal, complete-partial,* and *finished-initial* ways of speaking. Formal refers to the style used in speeches, lectures, and sermons. Informal refers to the style used in everyday exchanges in the family, in school, and in business settings. Complete means that you are speaking in whole sentences and paragraphs; partial means that you are speaking in clipped or choppy phrases or words. Finished means that your material is carefully prepared and planned before you speak: we frequently refer to this type as prepared speech. In contrast, initial means that you speak without prior preparations: this is often referred to as impromptu speech.

Whether the speaking is formal or informal, it can be classified in more detail. As with writing, you can differentiate among *descriptive, analytical, critical-persuasive,* and *creative* types of speaking. Since these types are exactly the same as the types of writing, I shall make only one additional observation: although most people write only descriptively, most people use various ways of speaking quite frequently, probably because we develop the ability to speak long before we can write and because we use speech much more often than writing. As we shall see, this condition may retard your efforts to modify this self-demand. Certainly it means that it can make meeting course-demands much more difficult.

Relationship of Speaking to Course-Demands

There are several obvious relationships between speaking and typical course-demands. Regarding Regulations and Activities, many courses require formal oral presentations in the form of reports, speeches, or debates. Many also demand informal oral participation in answering questions or in a class discussion. Some courses even require oral instead of written examinations.

In addition, there are some course-demands that may be more subtle. For example, in some courses Teacher Evaluation does not openly include oral class participation, but the teacher does credit his students for good discussion without informing the class that he is doing this. Likewise, Student Pressure may be negative toward "eager" students who ask questions. Finally, in the area of the Professor's Personality, a particular teacher may be favorably disposed toward a student who can use critical-persuasive speaking effectively but react negatively to students who rely on clipped or choppy speech.

There can also be another indirect relationship between speaking and course-demands. As I have indicated above, you can use speaking to aid remembering. Thus, when a course-demand includes the ability to remember, speaking can be used to help meet that course-demand. This means that even in those courses that do not require direct speaking in the form of speeches or discus-

sion, you may need this ability to meet other course-demands.

Modifying Speaking as a Self-Demand

Modifying this self-demand involves the same steps that I have described for the other abilities. You must first determine how well you can perform this ability. While there are clinical methods to measure abnormal speech patterns, unfortunately there are no standardized tests that can be used for your purposes here; therefore, you have to rely on informal methods.

Despite this, you should be able to obtain a good estimate of your speaking ability in comparison with other people of your age. As I pointed out in Chapters IV and VI, you can use your High School Record, Non-School Activities, Significant Others, College Personnel, and College Record to give you some insights. For example, your achievement in high school and college English and speech courses reflects this to some extent. Further, your participation in extracurricular activities can indicate how comfortable you feel when speaking. Likewise your performance in an elected club position can give information. Certainly you should not overlook the judgments that your teachers make of your speaking ability.

Although the above information can be useful, you should realize that you may not be obtaining estimates of your ability to perform each of the various types of speaking. If you do not find out how well you can speak in a critical-persuasive or creative manner, for example, you may not get this kind of information until you take a college course whose goals include the development of these types of speaking. Discovering the level of your ability in each of these areas may come only as a result of trying to modify them.

Assuming that you have obtained this information, you are now faced with the task of modification. Because, as I indicated above, your speaking abilities have evolved from an early age, changing them requires considerable time and energy. Strong speech habits have formed that are difficult to modify. Therefore, perhaps the best way of changing is through formal speech courses. Most colleges today offer introductory as well as advanced courses. Such courses provide expert advice and practice in specific speaking abilities.

In addition some colleges offer speech clinics. These are especially helpful for certain speech conditions such as stuttering or speaking with a pronounced accent. Private tutoring for other modifications can also help. Frequently, the fear of giving speeches can be overcome in this manner. Working with the college counselor may also help with such problems, since these are often related to other psychological problems.

Finally, there are several methods of self-help that can be beneficial. By using a tape recorder you can practice speaking and then hear how you sound to others. Practicing speeches in this manner can be especially valuable. Likewise, if the professor is willing, you can record class discussions and then listen to yourself speak in comparison with your classmates. Along the same line, you can record discussions with friends to get further data and practice. To gain maximum benefit from such procedures, you should also use one or more manuals or books on improving speech. Several good ones that give specific instructions are available. I have listed some of them at the end of this chapter.

CHAPTER SUMMARY

It is possible to modify remembering, writing, and speaking if you know which of these abilities are weak. To do this, you must be able to identify the different types of remembering, writing, or speaking which you use. Comparing these to the course-demands can then show which ones need modification. Because there are many practical, concrete means of practicing desired changes, you can usually change these abilities. In this chapter I have detailed some of these means. When you do make an effort to change one ability, it usually helps your efforts to modify the others.

THOUGHT QUESTIONS

1. What is the major difference between recall and recognition as types of remembering? Which of these is required most by your course-demands?
2. How can reading, listening, and questioning help remembering? How can you use this information to modify your remembering ability?
3. Which types of writing are most difficult for you? Why? How can you change this?
4. How can writing and speaking aid remembering? Which types of writing and speaking can most help your ability to remember?
5. What kinds of speaking do your course-demands require? If you are weak in these, how can you modify your ability?

SELECTED REFERENCES

Modifying Remembering

Farquhar, William W., and others. *Learning to Study.* New York: Ronald Press, 1960. Chapter 5.

Morgan, Clifford T., and Deese, James. *How to Study.* New York: Mc-Graw-Hill, 1957. Chapter 3.

Voeks, Virginia. *On Becoming an Educated Person,* rev. ed. Philadelphia: Saunders, 1964. Chapter 3.

Modifying Writing

Flesch, Rudolf, and others. *How to Become a Better Student.* New York: Sterling, 1957. Chapter 3.

Ruchlis, Hy. *Clear Thinking.* New York: Harper, 1962. Chapter 4.

Wedeen, Shirley U. *College Remedial Reader.* New York: Putnam, 1958. Chapter 13.

Modifying Speaking

Hanlon, Willa N. *What Good Is English?* Chicago: Science Research Associates, 1956. Chapters 1–6.

Sondell, Bess. *How to Be a Better Speaker.* Chicago: Science Research Associates, 1950. Chapters 1–6.

Wedeen, Shirley U. *College Remedial Reader.* New York: Putnam, 1958. Chapters 11, 12.

CHAPTER XII

Abilities: Problem-Solving, Integrating, and Creating

We now come to the abilities that are most difficult to modify. Problem-solving, integrating, and creating are very dependent on biologically inherited potential and certain personality characteristics. In addition, they require high levels of achievement in the other abilities discussed in the previous chapters. For maximum understanding of this section, therefore, you should relate the following material to our earlier discussions.

PROBLEM-SOLVING

The Nature of Problem-Solving

Problem-solving refers to the process involved in arriving at the correct or best answer to a *specific problem for which you previously did not have a solution.* This definition requires some explanation. If you have a problem, this means you are confronted with conditions or information stated in the form of a question whose solution requires more than recall or recognition. Thus, the solution usually demands, in addition to remembering, a reorganization of what is remembered. It may also require new perceptions of what is remembered. Further, it may require the application of remembered formulas, equations, and so on. The solution, in addition, may also depend upon two other abilities that we shall look at shortly: integrating and creating.

Carrying out problem-solving involves

the use of various abilities. Remembering is basic. Depending upon the problem you wish to solve, however, intellectual problem-solving can also require reading, listening, questioning, writing, and speaking. A high level of problem-solving ability is dependent upon adequate abilities in these other areas.

You probably have already noted another aspect of problem-solving: it is a way of learning. Thus, you can view problem-solving as either an ability or a way of learning. In fact, if you have a high ability to solve problems, you probably learn easily.

This discussion also implies that there are typically several steps or processes involved in problem-solving. First, you must understand the nature of the problem that confronts you. Second, you must remember the information, formula, or equation that is applicable to the problem. Third, for some problems there must be a reorganization or new perception of what you recall or recognize. Fourth, for some problems there must be an integration of the newly organized or perceived material. Finally, for some problems there must be the creation of new information or conditions. It should be clear that the nature of the problem dictates the steps that it will be necessary to follow in solving it. It also controls what other abilities (reading, writing, and so on) must be used.

As you might guess, there are different types of problem-solving; these are primarily intellectual, social, or physical. Intellectual problem-solving means the solution depends mainly on the use of your mind. Social problem-solving means that the solution depends mainly on the use of the non-intellectual aspects of your personality (emotions, needs, and so on). Physical problem-solving means the solution depends mainly on the use of your body.

Finding solutions to problems frequently involves more than one type of problem-solving. Figuring out a mechanical puzzle usually requires the coordination of the mind and body. Finding a suitable friend for a party demands the use of both the mind and the personality. Obtaining academic success, of course, requires solving problems that are primarily intellectual; hence this type of problem-solving is most frequently required by course-demands.

Relationship of Problem-Solving to Course-Demands

Courses differ widely in the amount of problem-solving they require. Some, for example introductory history courses, typically do not involve problem-solving. Others, such as mathematics, are almost entirely built about this concept. A few, such as economics or psychology, tend to require some problem-solving. Beyond these differences, course-demands differ even more in terms of the specific types of intellectual problem-solving required. Some involve primarily verbal language (philosophy), whereas others require primarily non-verbal language (chemistry). Some require mainly the applications of laws (physics), while some demand mainly the applications of principles (art). Regardless of the subject matter, meeting course-demands during the junior and senior years of college does involve more of this ability than the first two years.

Even as a freshman, however, you probably need this ability to carry out certain Activities. Preparing certain English themes, writing philosophy term papers, or preparing speech lectures may require problem-solving. Doing chemistry laboratory assignments, psychology experiments, or accounting projects may also demand this. Certainly examinations in some subjects depend on problem-solving ability. Mathematics, economics, and physics are prime examples.

Modifying Problem-Solving as a Course-Demand

Modifying this self-demand, in contrast to most of the other abilities we have looked at, is extremely difficult, primarily because intellectual problem-solving is very dependent upon several personality characteristics that are very much emotionally charged. Further, this ability is dependent upon several other abilities. Changing your problem-solving ability requires changing these other characteristics and abilities.

Let me explain this point more fully. If you are faced with a problem in a course, you must first be able to understand the problem. Usually this means you have to be able to recall other information related to this problem; thus, you must be able to remember well. Then you have to relate this information (say an economics principle) to the data of the problem. If the selected principle does not give you a solution, you may have to reorganize the data of the problem. Perhaps you will need recall and the use of another principle. These steps require a certain amount of flexibility (a personality characteristic) in moving from one view of the data to another and in giving up one identified principle to select a different one. All of these processes, moreover, occur in the mind, and, therefore, require considerable ability to think abstractly and/or to handle concepts involving spatial relations, both abilities which are, to a considerable extent, genetically determined.

Although problem-solving is difficult to modify, there are some very good methods available for estimating the level of your ability. As part of most intelligence tests, there are some subtests that measure abstract and spatial-relations reasoning. As a result, you can determine how you compare to other students of your age on these characteristics. There are also some special aptitude tests that get at these and other problem-solving aspects. Once again, you can get this information by talking to your college counselor who probably has these data from the high school or college testing programs. If not, he can arrange for such tests.

In addition, there are several informal ways of estimating this ability. Throughout high school most students have taken various courses that require problem-solving. By identifying those courses that included considerable amounts of this type of thinking,

you can get a rough idea of your ability in this area by noting your level of achievement. You should keep in mind that these grades are influenced by many other factors and, thus, provide only a rough estimate. Nevertheless, if you discover that you do much better in courses that require only recall and recognition, you might conclude that you are weak in this ability.

You should also notice those courses in which you do your best problem-solving. Because there are different kinds of problem solving, you must see if you tend to do better in one area or another. For example, you may discover that you have high ability in solving non-verbal problems (mathematics) but are poor in solving verbal problems (social studies). Likewise you may be good at applying laws (physics) but poor in reorganizing information (history).

Another informal method is for you to compare the way you do your problem-solving assignments with the methods which your friends and classmates use. This is usually possible because the teachers in these kinds of courses often go over in class the solutions to assigned problems.

Once you have been able to estimate your level of ability for the various types of problem-solving, you are faced with the task of modification. Assuming that your genetic inheritance and personality characteristics do not greatly limit possibilities for change (and they might), there are several steps you can follow.

First, you can, on your own, practice problem-solving. To be valuable, however, this step should follow the process I described above. If you are deficient in any of the other required abilities (reading, writing, and so on), they must be modified first. Thus, if you cannot read well analytically you must correct this; likewise, if you have poor recall of required principles or laws, you must improve in this area first.

As part of this practice, you must also try to reorganize information, to put it in a different order or grouping. Along with this, you must try to perceive the information in different ways. An example may help to clarify these ideas.

Problem:

How many faces are there in this figure?

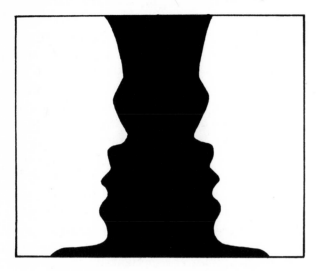

What solution did you come to? None; one; two? Your answer depends upon how you viewed this figure. It also depends upon the way in which you recall the word "face." You could say none, since you see only a black vase. However, you could say one or two if you see a white profile of a face (mouth wide open!) on the left and/or right sides of the figure. It is this kind of reorganization and perception of information that must be practiced. In addition, you must practice integrating and creating. I shall explain ways of doing this in the following sections.

Besides self-practice, there is a second method of modifying your problem-solving ability. Because certain courses tend to emphasize this ability, signing up for these courses will force you to work at solving problems. You should realize, of course, that you will probably not receive high grades; however, exposing yourself to formal teaching which demands this ability is a valuable procedure in helping you to develop it. This can also make it possible to work with the instructor individually. If you sign up for introductory rather than advanced courses of this nature, it will make this procedure easier; basic courses in literature, accounting, psychology, sociology, philosophy, or mathematics will probably provide you with an opportunity to develop your problem-solving ability.

Another possible method for modification is to work with a special tutor. He can be a more advanced student or a classmate who has a high level of problem-solving ability. Perhaps he can help most by offering to explain how he solves problems.

You can see from this discussion that there are fewer ways of modifying this self-demand than the others we discussed earlier. However, reading several references on problem-solving may further help you; the ones listed at the end of this chapter have been selected with this goal in mind. If these various methods do not work for you, discussing this problem with your college counselor may help you understand the reasons why they do not, and it may also help you to plan what to do in view of this limitation. A number of alternatives are available: they range from staying with a course and doing poorly to changing courses, curricula, or colleges.

INTEGRATING

The Nature of Integrating

Integrating is another mental ability that is comparatively difficult to modify. I think you will see why after I explain what it is. *It is the process of finding relationships in materials previously perceived as unrelated.* Stating it another way, it is the process of fitting together two or more different things that earlier you have not seen as fitting together. You can integrate various kinds of material: isolated facts, different groups of facts, questions, rules, principles, formulas, equations, and laws.

In order to integrate different materials certain processes must typically occur. First you must discover common elements. This means you must be able, usually through association and recall, to see some relationship between the two sets of material. Thus, if you are going to integrate two historical facts, you must identify some direct or indirect connection between the two. For example, you are able to integrate the American and French Revolutions by recalling that each, in its own way, represented a throwing-off of a strong, centralized, inherited system of government.

A second process also helps integration. This is the placing of different materials in some hierarchy or order. One becomes more important, larger, or precedes the other. Thus, you can order the American and French Revolutions by date, by the amount of bloodshed, or by the number of people involved; this ordering provides ways to build a ladder between the two different sets of materials.

Reorganization of perception is a third process frequently required in achieving integration. This means one set of materials may have to be perceived differently before its elements can be related to the other materials. In the above example, you may have to change your perception of the American Revolution; this may mean looking at it from the European viewpoint in contrast to the American. As a result, you may see that it was only one of many problems that England faced at the time, and that France's sympathetic support of the Colonists was related to her difficulties with England. Thus, the American Revolution has a different meaning to the French people. This condition later had significance for the emergence of their own revolution.

From this discussion of the processes involved in integration, you can see that this ability is quite similar to certain types of problem-solving. In fact, as I pointed out earlier, integrating is required to solve some mental problems. This is particularly true when the problems involve highly abstract, verbal (non-mathematical) elements. In this sense, integrating and problem-solving can be the same. As we shall see shortly, the same close relationship also exists between integrating and creating.

Relationship of Integrating to Course-Demands

The similarity between the abilities to integrate and to solve problems helps to explain the relationship of this self-demand to course-demands. As with problem-solving, the closest relationships occur in advanced college courses. Not too many introductory courses require the student to integrate the subject matter; by contrast recall and recognition (remembering) are more often demanded.

Perhaps the most frequent use of integrating, in the first two years of college, is in the humanities and social science courses. Even here, however, integration is not typically required by most Regulations and Activities. Although high achievement in these courses may demand the integration of material in papers, class discussion, and examinations, students can gain average grades without displaying this ability.

Although the use of integrating is typically not built into freshman course-demands, it is an extremely important ability because it can greatly aid the achievement of other course-demands. I have already noted that remembering can be aided by writing and problem-solving. This is also true for integrating. Here is how this occurs.

You recall that one way by which you remember is through association. You can, therefore, understand that the more similar the items are, the easier it is to associate them. Hence, it is easier to recall "hat" if you have associated it with "coat" than if you have associated it with "refrigerator." Likewise, you can recall an economics principle more easily if you associate it with some real business experience than with a biological experiment.

Integrating helps remembering in the same way. It produces similarities between two elements that, at first glance, have nothing in common. Thus, using our historical example, you can better remember various aspects of the American and French Revolutions after you have integrated them, because the integration has given *structure* to the various facts or aspects that previously were isolated. As you recall one or more aspects, the others are quickly connected in your mind because they are part of the same structure. This process is similar to a chain reaction. Once one part of a line of dominoes has fallen, for example, the rest fall in line. Once you recall one similarity between the American and French Revolutions, the other common elements are also recalled.

Integrating can also help you achieve other course-demands in the same way. It is easier to read when you see that the material has some structure. This is particularly true for analytical, interpretive, and critical reading. If you can integrate various sections of a chapter or book, you will be better able to understand the separate parts.

Writing can be improved through the same process. If you can show the relationships of the various ideas you write about, the material is clearer and, thus, the resulting piece of work is better. This is true for both complete and partial writing. Note-taking is an excellent example of the latter. Hence, if your class notes are integrated and show relationships, they will be easier to understand and remember. You can integrate them by using an outline or coded system whereby the different ideas are connected.

Listening, questioning, and speaking can also be aided in this manner. Listening to a lecture is facilitated when you can connect the ideas through integration. This illustrates well why listening, as I pointed out earlier, must be an active process. Questioning also becomes easier because you can think of questions that will help you understand several ideas. In fact, when you don't see relationships in separate ideas, you can use this condition as a sign that you must ask questions. Speaking can be helped in the same way. Before you speak on a topic, it is help-

ful if you know how it is related to other material. In this way you can better explain to your audience the particular meaning you are giving your subject.

These various examples should make it clear to you that the ability to integrate is very important. Its importance for freshmen does not lie so much in its direct relationship to course-demands but in its significance in carrying out the other self-demands required in college.

Modifying Integrating as a Self-Demand

Because of its importance, it would be nice if the ability to integrate could be easily modified. The truth is, however, that the ability to integrate cannot be easily changed, because of the same factors that prevent easy modification of your problem-solving ability. Both depend upon several characteristics that are highly determined by genetic factors as well as certain personality traits that are fairly fixed. Integration of abstract facts, principles, or equations, of course, depends upon a high level of abstract thinking, based on both verbal and non-verbal material. It also depends upon a flexibility of perception that is very influenced by your personality pattern.

Estimating your ability to integrate, therefore, can be done in exactly the same way that you estimated your problem-solving ability. You can use test data, your past achievement in various courses requiring considerable integration, and comparisons of your ability with that of your classmates.

Similarly, the limited means for modifying this self-demand follow those described for problem-solving. You can use self-practice, taking courses requiring this ability, and special tutoring.

Despite this situation, there is one type of integration that is more subject to modification: this is integration of descriptive and factual information. Because integration of this material can be achieved by merely ordering it in some way, learning to order information can help you develop this ability. The ordering of such material is most easily accomplished by putting it into an outline. By definition, an outline puts separate pieces of information in some order in relation to each other. Thus, "I" is higher than "A," and "1" is higher than "a," and so on.

Fortunately, most students can learn to develop outlines. When you lack this ability, there are several procedures you can follow. Because many freshman English courses require that you do this prior to writing themes, you can use this course to get help. Many speech courses also require outlining. In addition, many colleges offer "How to Study" courses and clinics that emphasize this ability. Finally, various study guides are available that give specific instructions and practice in outlining. I have listed several of these at the end of this chapter. The chapters by Morgan and Deese and Voeks in their books should be especially helpful.

CREATING

The Nature of Creating

The last ability that I shall discuss, creating, is also the most difficult to modify, because this self-demand requires high levels of ability in problem-solving and integrating. If you lack these two abilities, the chances are very high that you will not be able to modify your present ability to create. This should be clearer after I explain the nature of creating.

Stated simply, *creating is the process of developing something new*. It can involve developing new scientific hypotheses, principles, equations, formulas, laws, methods, or applications. Along humanistic lines, it can be producing new prose, poetry, painting, sculpture, or developing new interpretations of these art forms. It can also be developing new methods or applications of the above forms. In other words, creating can take various forms—from the highly abstract to the highly concrete.

To create, you typically begin with a problem that you are trying to solve. If your problem-solving ability is high enough, you not only solve the problem but you also create a solution which is new. All problem-solv-ing does not lead to creating, but usually creating comes out of problem situations. Since integrating is frequently required in problem-solving, creating usually involves some type of integration, too.

This can be seen quite clearly in poetry-writing. The "problem" here might be the poet's desire to express his feelings about a great military victory. The problem involves a decision about what form to use. Its solution will depend upon the poet's integration of his feelings with the historical event. Creating the poem, then, will be the result of his attempts to "sense" his feelings and express them in an appropriate poetic form.

Creating in the scientific realm usually follows the same process. Discovering the cause of cancer, for example, would depend upon problem-solving and integrating abilities. In this case, however, creating will depend less on the personal, subjective experience and more on the objective, external manipulation of conditions. In either case, though, the creation comes out of a new perception of the existing conditions.

Relationship of Creating to Course-Demands

As you might guess, there is not a great demand for creating in the first two years of college. On the contrary, most courses require that you remember existing knowledge rather than create any new interpretations, principles, and so on. Perhaps the major exception is courses in English literature. Some professors of literature courses require that you create short stories, poems, or sonnets. Likewise, painting, sculpture, and ceramics courses may involve this ability. This is certainly not the case in most natural and social science courses: in fact, the student who develops a new theory or principle will probably find his behavior unacceptable to his professor!

Although the situation may not change radically during the junior and senior years, some creating is usually demanded by more courses. This is especially true in literature, philosophy, music, and art courses. It may even be true for honors seminars in the natural and social sciences.

Modifying Creating as a Self-Demand

Although creating is not an ability that is frequently required in most college courses, it can be helpful to have some estimate of your ability to create. This knowledge may not help you greatly to modify this self-demand, but it can be beneficial in selecting subjects. Therefore, I shall briefly discuss here ways of estimating this ability.

Perhaps the simplest means is by self-analysis. If you look at your experiences in those high school and college courses that have required some creating, you can see how well you have been able to create in the past. These courses have probably been in English, art, music, or philosophy. However, in order to make this analysis, you will have to think about each course and evaluate the type of Activities required. Looking at the course grade is not enough, since there may have been only one or two Activities that required creating. You will have to identify these and see how well you did there.

In addition, you can also analyze your non-school experiences. As I indicated in Chapter VI, these may include club, home, camp, and similar situations. Since they typically require different kinds of creating, your experiences there will give you a different type of knowledge. Combined with your school experiences, you should be able to get a fairly good estimate of your ability to create.

This estimate can then be checked by several methods. One is to obtain the evaluations of instructors who know you well. Because they can compare you with many other students, they can help to make your estimate more objective. A second procedure is to use psychological testing. This is not easy to do, since tests for creativity have only recently been developed. Accordingly, your counselor may not have available the necessary data for comparing your scores with those of other students who have been cre-

ative. Taking such a test, however, can give you a rough estimate of how difficult you find this type of test. In the final analysis, however, the best way of determining your creative ability is to see how well you can perform in situations that demand creating. In college this means taking courses that require it.

Although this may prove frustrating and lead to non-success, this method is probably also the best way of attempting to modify your ability to create. If any change is to occur, it will probably happen only under careful supervision by an instructor who requires creativity. A course so designed, such as creative writing, can tell you how well you can create with a certain kind of subject matter and, at the same time, indicate how much modification you can hope to achieve.

One last thought about this self-demand. Because it is an ability that is much more complex than any of the others, this brief discussion may not have given you any real understanding of it. Therefore, I have included in the list of readings at the end of this chapter several more thorough treatments. Although they are somewhat technical, I think you will find them enlightening.

CHAPTER SUMMARY

Problem-solving requires finding solutions and, as such, it is required in certain college courses. Although it depends upon remembering, the latter is not enough. Because there are different types of problem-solving, modifying this ability requires different activities, depending on the type involved. We can say the same for integrating and creating. In fact, these three types of abilities greatly depend upon and are furthered by each other. Modifying them, therefore, is easier for persons who tend to handle one or more of them well. Although integrating and creating are not frequently required in undergraduate courses, having these abilities can make the difference between average and outstanding academic success.

THOUGHT QUESTIONS

1. What steps are usually involved in problem-solving? Knowing this, in what ways can you modify your ability?
2. To what extent is problem-solving ability required by your course-demands? What implication does this have for your ability level?
3. In what ways can you use integrating to aid you in remembering, writing, and speaking? Why is this so?
4. What kinds of college courses usually require creating? How could you use this information to increase your ability to create? Do you think this is possible? Why?
5. In what ways are your problem-solving, integrating, and creating abilities similar? Do you think you can modify your levels of these abilities? Why?

SELECTED REFERENCES

Modifying Problem-Solving

Dudycha, George J. *Learn More with Less Effort.* New York: Harper, 1957. Chapters 3, 15.

Garrison, Roger H. *The Adventure of Learning in College.* New York: Harper, 1959. Chapter 8.

Lindgren, Henry C. *Psychology of Personal and Social Adjustment,* rev. ed. New York: American, 1959. Chapter 15.

Modifying Outlining

Farquhar, William W., and others. *Learning to Study.* New York: Ronald Press, 1960. Chapter 7.

Morgan, Clifford T., and Deese, James. *How to Study.* New York: McGraw-Hill, 1957. Chapter 5.

Voeks, Virginia. *On Becoming an Educated Person,* rev. ed. Philadelphia: Saunders, 1964. Chapter 2.

Modifying Creating

Cronbach, Lee J. *Educational Psychology,* rev. ed. New York: Harcourt Brace, 1963. Chapter 11.

Dudycha, George J. *Learn More with Less Effort.* New York: Harper, 1957. Chapters 3, 6.

Rogers, Dorothy. *The Psychology of Adolescence.* New York: Appleton-Century-Crofts, 1962. Chapter 5.

CHAPTER XIII

Types of Learning

You recall that we have already discussed the types of learning in various sections of Chapters IV and VI. In Chapter IV, I described in some detail how we use *trial and error, rote, association, conscious problem-solving,* and *unconscious insight.* I also indicated that different courses may require greater use of one of these types of learning, and, in illustration, I compared a psychology and an English course. In Chapter VI, I explained how you can determine the type(s) of learning you prefer and can do well. Thus, in this section, I shall concentrate on explaining the ways you can modify your pref-

erences for, and ability to use, the various types of learning. Before proceeding with this topic, therefore, I suggest you review the material presented in Chapters IV and VI.

WAYS OF MODIFYING PREFERENCES FOR DIFFERENT TYPES OF LEARNING

Your preference for one or more types of learning can be subjected to careful analysis, and changing your preferences is usually possible. On the other hand, because your preferences typically are habitual, they tend to resist modification. These two points mean that you can change your preferences, but only as a result of considerable effort. Let's look at the steps that can be followed. First, you must determine the type or types that you prefer. (You have seen how to do this from the discussion in Chapters IV and VI.) Second, you must ask why you have this preference. As you might guess, your previous school experiences are very influential here. If you prefer rote you probably developed it because your teachers emphasized this type of learning. On the other hand, you may prefer conscious problem-solving because you obtained your greatest academic success when using this approach.

The third step involves finding out that other types of learning can be used. Obviously, you have already done this. However, it should not surprise you to learn that many college students are unaware that there are ways of learning other than the one they have always used: finding out about other types is most important for them. The fourth step, and a very crucial one, involves finding satisfaction from using another type of learning. You can understand the significance of this when you recall that your preferences are typically habitual. Changing them is like changing habits. You must be able to obtain or expect satisfaction from using the new type of learning before you are willing to give up using the old type.

Finally, you must realize that different types of learning are more suitable for certain learning situations. Until you really understand this, you may prefer one type because you think it is equally good for all courses.

Notice that I have been discussing modifying *preferences* for types of learning. As you know, preferences are not the same as abilities. Thus, we must now look at the possibilities for *changing your ability to use* different types of learning. To do this, I shall take each type of learning and discuss its relationship to course-demands. Then, I shall indicate the various means available for modifying your ability to use it.

TRIAL AND ERROR

Relationship to Course-Demands

As you will recall, trial and error learning is very commonly used in everyday life. Because it is usually the *least efficient* means of learning, however, you might imagine that it is not required by most courses. This is true. Nevertheless, there are certain times when trial and error learning is demanded. This occurs when you are given a problem to solve on your own and you have no previously learned laws, formulas, or principles to apply to it.

Although this situation does not usually occur in freshman or sophomore courses, it may be present in advanced courses, particularly if they require independent research work. In this situation, before problem-solving learning can be applied, you may have to test, in a hit-and-miss fashion, your own ideas. After this initial learning, you can then approach the problem with a more systematic, problem-solving approach.

This discussion points out an interesting phenomenon. Although your courses do not usually require you to use trial and error, many students use it in attempting to succeed in their college work. This is probably simply a carry-over of habitual behaviors developed in high school. Unless you find academic success by using other types of learning to solve your problem of non-success, you will continue your habit.

Modifying Trial and Error Learning

I have just suggested the means that must be used if you are to modify your ability to use trail and error learning. You must know that there are other ways of learning and then attempt to use them. Since most people already use rote and association, this should not prove to be a problem.

The one problem that may arise, however, is that you may not use trial and error when you should! As I indicated above, this approach can be useful at times. If the course-demands include it, but you refuse to behave in this way, you may not be able to succeed in a task. For example, this could result in a failure to succeed in a research project that cannot be solved by previously established means. Avoiding this kind of behavior depends upon a flexible approach to learning. This, of course, suggests the importance of personality needs. Modifying your ability to use trial and error, then, can be helped by appropriate personality needs.

ROTE

Relationship to Course-Demands

In contrast to trial and error, rote learning is very frequently included in course-demands, and this is particularly true of basic or introductory courses. Because these courses typically present many new concepts and vocabulary words that are essential to any understanding of the subject matter, you are required to recognize and recall them. Since these concepts and words are new to you, you must fix them in your memory in about the same manner that a child learns language: repetition, repetition, repetition. Following this, you can associate new concepts and words with those already recalled.

Modifying Rote Learning

As with the other self-demands, in order to use rote learning, you must be aware of the way you use it. Through self-observation you can easily determine this. Simply think about the ways you have used rote learning in the past. You can mark down the typical times as well as the situations for which you use it. Keeping a written log for a week can help you to be sure that you are viewing your behavior accurately.

You can also indicate *how* you learn by rote—by internal verbal repetition, external verbal repetition, written repetition, or any combination of the three. *Internal verbal* refers to repeating the material to yourself (not out loud) over and over again. *External verbal* refers to repeating the material out loud, to yourself or to another person, over

and over again. *Written* refers to repeating the material in writing over and over again.

As you might guess, using a *combination* approach usually produces the best rote learning. With a combination approach, you will say the material silently to yourself, say it out loud, and then write it as you say it. You can also add the technique of viewing the material as you say it, by using *flash cards*. In this case, you will flash the question or new word (written on a small card) quickly to yourself; if you do not recall the answer or correct associated word, you can look at the opposite side of the card for the answer. We have already seen why these combinations should produce the quickest rote learning. Using speaking, writing, and viewing enhances your concentration and also brings into play additional senses (seeing, hearing, feeling).

Once you have determined the ways in which you have been using rote, you can proceed to the next step—deliberate practice in using the other methods which you have not been using. If you have not used written repetition, you could try that; if you have not used a combination, you could try it too.

Keep in mind that I am discussing the modification of rote learning and not referring to any other learning method. Accordingly, you may discover from self-analysis that you are already using the various methods of rote learning, and, thus, you may not have to improve this method. Rather you will have to turn to the other types of learning. You must be flexible enough in your use of rote to apply the other types when necessary. Once again we see how personality needs, attitudes, and habits can influence your attempts to modify this self-demand.

ASSOCIATION

Relationship to Course-Demands

We saw above that rote can be used to learn the fundamental concepts and vocabulary that are essential to most courses. Actually, as I have implied, association is also used in rote learning. Before you can use repetition, the material has to be connected to something: "table" has to be connected to "tableau"; "equal" to "="; "water" to "H₂O."

In addition to this method, association can be used to aid recall and recognition in another way. You have already seen how speaking and writing can aid remembering. Other senses (hearing and feeling) became involved, so that you associate the sound and touch sensations with the abstract symbol that you are trying to recall. In this case you have an *association of an abstract concept with a physical sensation.* The two types of content are recalled together. You have seen this principle applied in the combination type of rote learning.

There is another way that you can use association to aid remembering. You can associate some *unusual* person, place, thing, or action with the material you want to recall. Very often this is done by creating some peculiar combination that will stand out because of its uniqueness. For example, remembering the spaces on the *G* musical staff is easier if you imagine that they are parts of the *face* of the music page. Thus, the spaces spell out FACE. You can also help yourself to remember dates, places, and people in the same manner.

As you might guess from these uses, association, like rote, is very crucial to meeting course-demands. In addition to aiding remembering, however, it can help problem-solving, integrating, and creating. When these abilities are required, associating known material with the new or unknown helps. *You should note here that association represents an approach to learning that can be quite different from rote.* To aid problem-solving, integrating, and creating, there must be a freer or *more flexible* type of thinking than is involved in rote. To solve a problem, for example, may require several "free associations" rather than an exact one, in the sense of rote recall. You may have to try several associations before you begin to solve

the problem. This is particularly true for the social sciences where several theories might be used to approach a problem.

Modifying Association Learning

If you wish to modify your ability to handle association learning, you must know when you use the various types of association learning. Self-analysis should be able to give you this information. By thinking about, or keeping a log of, the ways you use association, you can see if modification is necessary. If you do not use association as an aid to remembering, this immediately suggests a weakness. Once again, deliberate practice can be used to modify this. This will probably be most valuable if carried on in conjunction with rote learning. This procedure is especially good toward the middle or the end of a course. By then the basic vocabulary has been mastered; new content can then be associated with the earlier material.

Once this has occurred, this type of association can be used to aid integration. As we saw earlier in Chapter XII, this kind of association facilitates the integration of different content. In other words, integrating can also give practice in associating.

Practice will also help you modify the way you use association in problem-solving. Although this use is not particularly subject to change, you can make some efforts to change it. In this instance you can attempt to "free associate" when faced with a problem by letting your mind wander and catch onto any idea that comes along. The assumption is that you will begin to recall or associate some past fact, law, or concept that is related to the problem. In this way, you stumble upon the way to solve the problem.

As you might guess, conscious desire to free associate may not work. Because of your habits, attitudes, personality needs, and other unconscious factors, you may not be able to let your mind wander. However, unless you attempt to do this, you will not know whether you can use association in this manner.

CONSCIOUS PROBLEM-SOLVING

Relationship to Course-Demands

We have already discussed in Chapters XI and XII how the abilities to remember and solve problems can be aided by using the conscious problem-solving type of learning. ince one or both of these abilities are required in most subjects, you can see that this approach to learning has a close relationship to most course-demands. If you are approaching learning in this way, you will deliberately follow a plan of action to solve a problem. You have to think up a way of trying to solve the problem before you actually try any solutions. Thus, this type of learning is quite different from rote and association.

It requires that you first identify the problem. Learning occurs as you try to follow the plan of action which you have drawn up. The learning can involve the solution itself or be a by-product of the process of trying to find the solution. Here are two examples of how this can occur. Let's go back to my earlier illustration of the American and French Revolutions: Let's assume your teacher wants you to learn (remember) the facts of the revolutions, so that you can understand the connections between the two (integration). If the teacher requires the use of conscious problem-solving learning, he may give an assignment such as the following: "Construct a chart that will show the similarities and differences between the American and French Revolutions. After you have done this, use this information to explain why you think (do not think) these two revolutions were closely related."

In order to complete this assignment, you will have to figure out a plan of attack, carry it out, and write up your conclusions. Assuming that the answer is not easily obtainable in a textbook or encyclopedia, you will have to use several references before coming up with your solutions. The finished chart and written answer can then be easily used, if necessary, to assure recall and recognition. Rote or association types of learning can be used to achieve this.

We see in this example that the professor has established the problem to be solved. However, if you want to use this type of learning to help meet your course-demands, you can establish your *own* problems. You can establish a broad one, such as the above example, or a narrower one, more related to a specific reading assignment. In this sense you create one or more questions about the assignment that you will try to answer as you study the content. Instead of creating your own questions (problem), you can, of course, use the questions the author has listed at the end of the reading. As you find answers to these questions, you will be finding solutions to your problem. Again, you can use rote and association to assure recall if necessary.

This second illustration, I am sure, reminds you of the type of assignments that many teachers have given you. Notice, however, that *completing assignments may not lead to significant learning unless you want to solve the problem.* Carrying out an assignment to please a teacher or to "get it over with" results in minimal learning. To use conscious problem-solving effectively, you must have a desire to solve the problem. When you yourself have created it (rather than the teacher), the chances are better that learning will occur as you seek the solution.

This discussion points out that some course-demands can be met by using conscious problem-solving as a type of learning. Success, however, requires considerable involvement on your part. When this occurs, a high level of learning will usually take place, because your level of concentration is high and your various senses have become involved (seeing, hearing, feeling).

Modifying Conscious Problem-Solving Learning

The above examples point out how you can attempt to modify the way you use conscious problem-solving as a type of learning.

You must first know when and how you use this method. Self-analysis should give you a good estimate. You can think about, or keep a log of, the times that you use it, and you should also notice who sets the problem, under what circumstances you try to solve it, and what results you achieve. Such data should also point out clearly your reactions to doing this type of learning.

To increase its use you will consciously have to use it more often and in different ways. This means that you will have to take a "problem-centered" view of study. As does changing most other self-demands, changing this one requires practice and experiencing success with the new behaviors. The practice can occur as you do your regular assignments. Following the guidelines of the second example, you can establish problems or questions, seek solutions in the reading, and then use rote and association. You can also try other methods: have a classmate establish the problem, use the author's questions, or ask the instructor to establish a problem. Regardless of the specific procedure followed, the main task is to increase and improve the setting of problems and the finding of solutions.

Increasing your use of this type of learning can also be facilitated by reading and using other authors' ideas. Several writers have spelled out in considerable detail methods of raising questions and finding solutions. Typically they have also related this procedure to reading and note-taking. The books by Dudycha and Stephens listed at the end of this chapter are especially clear. In addition, I think you will find the book by Lindgren on the nature of problem-solving to be helpful.

UNCONSCIOUS INSIGHT

Relationship to Course-Demands

Before discussing the relationship of unconscious insight to course-demands, let me briefly summarize the nature of this type of learning. Its uniqueness requires careful explanation.

You will recall that I first discussed unconscious factors in Chapter II and then developed this point further in Chapters IV, VI, and VII. Putting all of this material together, you have come to realize that the unconscious part of your personality can significantly influence the kinds of success you desire, the way you go about trying to reach that success, and the way you interpret the results.

More specifically, your unconscious reactions to failure or anticipated failure can lead to inhibiting behaviors. The resulting fears, anxieties, or anger, for the most part, tend to interfere with learning. They can cause you to forget, become immobile, or use other defense mechanisms that prevent positive study.

Despite this negative picture, you can actually use your knowledge of these probable results to *facilitate* learning. This is where unconscious insight as an approach to learning comes in. This type of learning occurs when you are not consciously trying to learn. Rather, you deliberately avoid making efforts to learn. Then, at a later time, you will discover that you remember the information or have solved the problem.

You should now be able to understand why this can occur. A typical process might go like this: You are studying for a difficult exam. You are using conscious problem-solving, rote, and association types of learning. As the exam day approaches, you feel quite anxious about the probable results. As you try harder, you discover you can't remember what you are memorizing. You also discover that you can't solve problems that you could do during the semester. You get even more panicky. Instead of continuing to study for the exam, however, you take a break. After a while you study the assignments for another course that you can do easily. While reading that material, you suddenly discover that you can recall all the information you were memorizing earlier!

In this case, you are able to recall this information probably because you have reduced your anxiety over the anticipated failure. You have done this by consciously turning to something you can do well, so that you have positive emotional reactions. Under these conditions, your unconscious emotional reactions of fear are not dominant, and, accordingly, the thoughts you had when these emotions were present can now become conscious. At this point you suddenly find that you can recall the information.

This example points out quite clearly that unconscious insight can be *consciously* planned! In other words, you can deliberately use your knowledge of your unconscious. You can give your unconscious reactions a chance to "cool off," so that your conscious mind can operate. This is even more necessary when you are trying to solve a problem. As you become frustrated by not being able to solve it, your unconscious reactions take over. However, by leaving the problem and turning your mind to other concerns, insight can occur. The emotional blocks that prevented a solution before dissipate; this in turn allows your conscious mind to "see" the solution. Thus, unconscious insight occurs.

Turning then to the relationship of this type of learning to course-demands, you will see that unconscious insight can be appropriate whenever your efforts to learn are not fruitful. You can use it in carrying out various assignments; it is especially helpful when you are writing papers, solving problems, and taking exams.

Modifying Unconscious Insight Learning

As you might guess, changing your use of unconscious insight is not easy, because of your other self-demands, especially your personality needs and unconscious factors. Nevertheless, there are several practical things you can do that *may* help you use your unconscious reactions.

I already described one in the above example. You can temporarily stop studying material that is threatening to you. After allowing a period of time to pass and turning to other subjects or activities, you can return to the original material. If too much threat still exists, the technique will not help. In that case, you may have to accept a lower level of success or drop the course. Talking to a counselor about the difficulty might also help at that point.

One other method may help to modify this self-demand. Since insights into problems can occur while you are doing other things you should learn to use these insights whenever they occur. By contrast, some students ignore these occurrences and treat them as intrusions upon their current activities. Instead, you should write down these ideas whenever they come to mind and use them later when you are studying that material again.

Finally, you may gain further understanding of the use of the unconscious in learning by reading several references. You might look over the list at the end of Chapter II. In addition, the discussion of the unconscious by Dudycha should be valuable: his book is listed at the end of this chapter.

CHAPTER SUMMARY

You can identify the types of learning you prefer and you can modify them by conscious practice. Trial and error, rote, and association are the easiest to change. Conscious problem-solving and unconscious insight tend to resist modification, since they are more dependent upon personality characteristics and inherited biological conditions. You have also seen that the ways of modifying the types of learning are similar to those you would use to change abilities.

THOUGHT QUESTIONS

1. Why do most students rely on rote learning? When can this type of learning lead to lower academic success?

2. Under what conditions might trial and error learning be beneficial in meeting course-demands? When does its use lead to minimum learning?
3. Why is association learning important in introductory college courses? How does it differ from rote learning?
4. How often do you use conscious problem-solving as a type of learning when you are studying? Why?
5. Can association be used to aid unconscious insight learning? Why? Have you done this? Why?

SELECTED REFERENCES

Modifying Types of Learning

Dudycha, George J. *Learning More with Less Effort.* New York: Harper, 1957. Chapters 4–6.

Lindgren, Henry C. *Psychology of Personal and Social Adjustment,* rev. ed. New York: American, 1959. Chapter 16.

Stephens, J. M. *Educational Psychology,* rev. ed. New York: Holt, 1956. Part 3.

CHAPTER XIV

Increasing Your

Academic Success

In the last six chapters I have explained the various ways of modifying self-demands. Earlier, in Chapter VII, you have made a comparison of your course-demands and your self-demands. Now we are ready to discuss the specific ways in which your self-demands can be modified. I shall take the ideas presented in Chapters VIII through XIII and show how they apply to David and to those of his self-demands which need change. Then I shall explain how you can do the same for yourself. When you have finished this process, your level of academic success should have increased.

DAVID'S EFFORTS TO MODIFY HIS SELF-DEMANDS

David's identification of his self-demands were summarized in Chapter VI. The comparison of his self-demands with the course-demands of Psychology 20 appeared in Chapter VII. We were able to see which of his self-demands *most frequently fitted* his course-demands and which *did not fit* them.

All of this analysis pointed out to David that he would probably be able to succeed in Psychology 20. However, he also realized that he could *increase* his level of academic success by modifying several of his self-demands. Since David was eager to do so, he made deliberate efforts in this direction. He developed a plan of action. For each self-demand that did not fit the course-demands, he decided on specific steps to follow, using the help he received from our conferences. We discussed ideas similar to those presented in Chapters VIII through XIII. He listed these ideas on paper so that he could check his progress later. Figure 21 shows which of his self-demands need modification, the problems that exist, and his plan to modify this situation. He filled in this information in Columns (1a), (1b), and (2). After he tried to carry out his plan, he analyzed the degree of benefit he had received. At that point, he marked down his conclusions. These are listed in Column (3).

There are several points you should notice about Figure 21. First, David listed his problems in Column (1b), deriving these statements from the data in Figures 16 and 19. He discovered his reasons and goals for going to college did not match the goals of Psychology 20, and this difference seemed to be the problem. David had to ask himself how he could change his goals. He thought about the difficulties in understanding his goals and the procedures he might use, and he then listed in Column (2) his plan of action. He made the same kind of analyses for the other self-demands.

A second point you should realize is that David's plan included a variety of procedures. He planned to read some special material, talk to several people, practice different ways of remembering, attend the reading clinic, study with a friend, practice taking breaks, practice using conscious problem-solving, and establish some new goals.

Notice a third point. These procedures were *consciously determined* to help modify one or more inappropriate self-demands. In other words, *David was using conscious problem-solving as a way of gaining higher academic success.* He was not using rote or association! He was learning how to succeed by carrying out a type of learning he did not normally use.

Fourth, you should realize that *not all of David's plan helped him.* Although he benefited considerably from analyzing his goals, talking to a counselor about his abilities, reading about methods of solving problems, practicing problem-solving learning, taking breaks, using several types of rote and association learning, and going to the reading clinic, other procedures did not work.

This partial failure illustrates that you should not expect this method of trying to increase your level of academic success to be completely effective. In fact, you should expect the reverse. You should anticipate some benefit from your first plan of action but realize that considerable benefit will come after revising this plan from time to time. As I pointed out at the end of Chapter IX, modifying self-demands is not a one-shot operation. It requires continuous appraisal and effort. In David's case, he was later able to increase his problem-solving ability and concentration habits so that he improved his academic success.

One final point should be mentioned. David had two self-demands that did not need modification—Personality Needs and Unconscious Factors—because these fitted the course-demands of Psychology 20. You should realize, however, that these two self-demands may not fit the demands of another subject. In that instance they too would need modification.

This should remind you again that maximum academic success depends upon your meeting the course-demands of *all of your courses.* For David this meant making an analysis of his other subjects and developing a plan of action for them when necessary.

MODIFYING YOUR SELF-DEMANDS

You are now ready to develop your own plan of action. Since you have already identified those of your self-demands that need modification, you need only to carry out the pro-

Figure 21 • **DAVID'S PLAN TO MODIFY HIS SELF-DEMANDS TO MEET THE COURSE-DEMANDS OF PSYCHOLOGY 20**

Self-Demand Needing Modification		Plan to Modify This Self-Demand (2)	Results of Attempts to Modify This Self-Demand (3)
Self-Demand (1a)	Problem (1b)		
Reasons and Goals (A)	My goals and course's goals differ	1. Think more carefully about my goals 2. Talk to advisor about purposes of college 3. Read information about how psychology can help in accounting 4. Talk to psychology majors regarding values of psychology 5. Try to determine additional goals for going to college	1. Now see that accountant can use psychology in meeting clients; also for getting along with his boss 2. Other efforts did not help at all 3. Set another goal for myself: learn precisely how psychology can be used by an accountant
Types of Abilities (B)	I have poor problem-solving ability, especially using abstract thinking	1. See my counselor; determine if I really have poor problem-solving ability 2. Read a book on methods of solving problems 3. Study with a friend who has this ability; ask him to help	1. Found out that I am poor in abstract problem-solving; same results as from high school testing 2. Discovered from book several ways of attacking problem; now trying out these ideas 3. Friend unwilling to study with me
Types of Learning (C)	I avoid using conscious problem-solving and unconscious insight as types of learning	1. Read some material on developing questions for study purposes 2. Practice using question-answer method of study 3. Read more about the nature of the unconscious 4. Practice taking breaks when I become frustrated while studying	1. Have learned to raise questions while studying; writing out answers helps but takes too long 2. Read material on unconscious; seems interesting but don't see how it can help me study 3. Taking breaks helps a lot: good idea!
Habits (D)	I can't concentrate for long and give up on hard assignments	1. Will try to use several types of rote and association learning 2. Try to analyze those times when I can't concentrate 3. Try to set immediate goals during study times	1. Using several types of rote and association help; saying the material out loud and using flash-cards keeps my mind on the material 2. Found out that I lose concentration most after studying for half an hour 3. Setting immediate goals doesn't seem to help
	I read poorly	1. Go to reading clinic on campus	1. Have increased speed and comprehension but still find some difficulty in reading 2. Trying to use new reading technique while studying
Attitudes (E)	I dislike non-practical subjects	1. Try to find some practical uses of psychology 2. Try to apply the content of this course to myself and accounting 3. Read material on importance of theory in understanding the world	1. See that psychology has some practical applications to accounting 2. Still find most of the course too theoretical 3. Still don't understand the importance of theory
Personality Needs (F)	None		
Unconscious Factors (G)	None		

cedures I have described above. Completing Activity Sheet 37 will help you to accomplish this.

Assuming that you have developed and carried out your plan of action, you will need to revise it to correct for errors. You will need to think of additional means of modifying your self-demands. If necessary, review Chapters VIII through XIII for ideas. Also consult your advisor and counselor. You may find it fruitful to reanalyze your course-demands and self-demands; this will probably provide new information for devising additional means of changing.

As you develop skill in carrying out these procedures, you will make fewer errors. Accordingly, figuring out your plans of action for your other courses should become easier, and, after you carry them out, your level of academic success should be higher.

REVIEWING THE PROCESS OF SUCCEEDING IN COLLEGE

I have now completed my discussion of the methods you can use to increase your success in college. Before finishing this chapter, however, I shall review for you the main points I have developed in this book. This review should help you to put into perspective the material you have just read. It should also help you understand better the relationships of the various ideas presented throughout the entire book. All of these points taken together represent the *process* of succeeding in college. For ease of comprehension I shall list them numerically.

1. *You and your college are unique.* We have noted that you, although similar to other students in some ways, are unique. You have a set of *self-demands* that represents your individuality. You must understand this uniqueness. Your college is also distinctive. It has many similarities to other colleges but it also has many different characteristics. While you are attending your college, you face a particular set of characteristics or requirements primarily coming from the courses you take. These requirements make up the *course-demands* you face. You must understand this uniqueness.

2. *There is no one method of succeeding suitable for all students.* Because students and their colleges are unique, no one method of trying to succeed will fit all students. Although common methods and procedures can be used, their usefulness will vary from student to student. This means you cannot rely upon a "canned" solution to your problems.

3. *Success depends primarily on you.* Because there is no one answer to all students' college problems, each student must find answers suitable to himself. This means that you must be involved in discovering the best solutions for you. You cannot depend entirely upon others. They can help you understand yourself and your college, but they cannot take your place. They can give you ideas, but *you* must evaluate their worth.

4. *You must compare your self-demands with your course-demands.* One of your crucial tasks is to compare your self-demands with your course-demands. As a result of this comparison, you can discover where these two sets of characteristics are similar and where they are different. You will know to what extent your reasons for going to college match the goals of the college. You will also know to what degree your abilities, types of learning, habits, attitudes, personality needs, and unconscious factors fit the requirements of your courses.

5. *You must decide if you want to change your self-demands and/or course-demands.* Once you have determined the extent to which you

and your courses are similar and different, you must decide what to do next. You may prefer to leave yourself as you are, change yourself, or change colleges. More specifically, this means you can leave your self-demands as they are, take the same courses, follow the same curriculum, and attend the same college. By contrast, you can attempt to change your self-demands, drop your courses, change majors, or drop out of or change colleges. You must choose among these various alternatives.

6. *Modifying your self-demands will require hard work.* If you decide to modify your self-demands, this will require hard work. In fact, you will probably have considerable difficulty in changing your unconscious factors, personality needs, and attitudes. Changing habits and goals will also prove difficult. Although you should be able to modify most of your abilities and types of learning, this too will require considerable time and effort. However, there are many ways of modifying them that can be used.

7. *You will probably need some help from others in modifying your self-demands.* As you attempt to modify yourself, you will probably need help from your college classmates, professors, advisor, and counselor. They can help you identify your self-demands and course-demands. They can also help you with ideas and supervision. In addition they can help you carry out your plan of action.

8. *Your success in college depends upon your continuous, deliberate efforts.* Even if others help you, *your* college success will depend upon *your* continuous, deliberate efforts. It is not enough to figure out and modify your self-demands once. This process must be an on-going one. For each new course this procedure must be repeated.

This last point summarizes well a basic theme of this book: Your success in college will probably require continuous and deliberate analysis, planning, and practice. Good luck!

GLOSSARY

ABILITY: The state of being able to perform a certain action or behavior because of genetic inheritance and/or some previous learning.

ACADEMIC SUCCESS: A high scholastic average or a high level of scholastic learning (without necessarily obtaining high grades) or both.

ANALYTICAL READING: Reading which provides comprehension of the main ideas, their relationships and their derivation, as well as a complete understanding of the material for later use or for the application of these ideas.

ANALYTICAL WRITING: Writing that shows the parts of something so that the reasons for its existence are depicted.

ANXIETY: A feeling that exists in the individual when he feels that his need satisfaction is being threatened.

ARTISTIC SUCCESS: Achievement attained by self-expression, through music, painting, sculpture, dancing, writing, drama, etc.

ASSOCIATION: A type of learning in which one thing is remembered by associating it with something that is already remembered; learning something new by connecting it with something already learned.

ATHLETIC SUCCESS: The achievement of the individual who becomes an outstanding player in a sport.

ATTITUDE: A predisposition to behave in a certain way.

ATTITUDE TOWARD AUTHORITY: The way the individual views people in authority positions: these might be teachers, policemen, supervisors, etc.

ATTITUDE TOWARD SEX AND MARRIAGE: The way the individual thinks and feels about sexual gratification and its relationship to marriage.

ATTITUDE TOWARD STUDY: The individual's willingness to carry out behaviors directed at gaining academic success.

ATTITUDE TOWARD OCCUPATIONAL CHOICE: The way an individual views the selection of an occupation and the importance it has for him.

ATTITUDE TOWARD PEERS: The way a student views other students attending college.

ATTITUDE TOWARD WORK: The way the individual views the labor involved in an occupation.

COLLEGE PERSONNEL: The various faculty members and staff available at a college: they can be instructors, dormitory advisors, health officers, academic advisors, counselors, financial-aid officers, deans, etc.

CONSCIOUS PROBLEM-SOLVING: A type of learning in which the individual learns something by deliberately following a plan of action to solve a problem.

COURSE-DEMANDS: The obvious and subtle requirements of courses: these may be Activities, Regulations, Goals, Types of Abilities, Types of Learning, Teacher Evaluation, Professor's Personality, and Student Pressure.

CREATIVE WRITING: The presentation of some idea, feeling, or attitude in a new and unique way; it may, although it does not always, analyze its subject, judge it, or try to convince others regarding it.

CRITICAL-PERSUASIVE WRITING: Writing which makes judgments about a subject and tries to convince others of these opinions.

CRITICAL READING: An evaluation of the true value or quality of a selection by going beyond the reading itself and, using certain standards, making a judgment about the selection.

DECEPTION: A defense mechanism in which the individual protects himself by fooling himself; he may do this by building excuses, seeing the other person as the culprit, logically proving to himself that he is correct, or forgetting his thoughts or feelings.

DEFENSE MECHANISMS: The unconscious thought processes which the individual uses to protect himself from unpleasant thoughts and feelings; these processes generally take one of three forms: substitution, deception, or withdrawal.

DESCRIPTIVE WRITING: Writing which describes or tells about an idea, feeling, or attitude: the idea can be about various things, people, places, conditions, or other ideas.

ECONOMIC SUCCESS: The ability to earn or accumulate enough money to purchase the goods and services desired.

EMPATHY: A positive feeling toward an individual accompanied by an understanding of how he thinks and feels.

FRUSTRATION-RELATED UNCONSCIOUS FACTORS: Feelings and processes that result when the individual's personality needs are threatened or are not satisfied.

GOALS: That which an individual strives to attain; there may also exist goals set by others (such as course goals) which the individual accepts as his and therefore strives to attain.

HABIT: A set way of doing something that is almost automatic.

HIGH SCHOOL RECORD: A listing of an individual's attainment in all facets of his high school experience, including both academic achievement and extra-curricular activities.

IDENTIFICATION: The pleasurable emotional experience of an individual who perceives that another person will, or is, satisfying his needs; it causes him to begin to move closer to that person psychologically; he becomes more like that person.

INDIVIDUALIZED STUDY: An individual's way of studying which he has established after making a thorough analysis of himself and his college.

INTEGRATING: The process of finding relationships in materials previously perceived as unrelated.

INTERPRETIVE READING: Reading in which the individual takes the ideas of a selection and determines their meaning for other ideas, events, problems, etc., going beyond the material presented and extrapolating the ideas of the selection.

INTERPRETIVE WRITING: Writing in which the individual goes beyond descriptive and analytical writing, trying to make some inferences or draw some conclusions beyond what an analysis of the material would give.

LEARNING: A change in behavior which is the result of some experience and not due to normal, physical growth: learning in college usually involves trial and error, rote, association, conscious problem-solving, or unconscious insight.

LISTENING: The ability to pay attention to sounds and noises in the environment: it can be superficial, analytic, interpretive, or critical.

MENTAL ABILITY: An ability that is primarily dependent upon the functioning of the mind.

MENTAL HABITS: Behaviors, carried out automatically, that are primarily based upon the mind and its intellectual processes.

NON-SCHOOL ACTIVITIES: Activities carried out in situations such as the home, social clubs, service organizations, informal peer groups, and religious groups.

OCCUPATIONAL SUCCESS: The individual's attainment of a high level of achievement in his chosen occupation.

PERSONALITY NEEDS: Biological and psychological forces within the individual that affect his behavior as they attempt to gain their own satisfactions.

PHYSICAL ABILITY: An ability that is primarily dependent upon the functioning of the body.

PHYSICAL HABITS: Behaviors, carried out automatically, that are primarily based upon the body and its movements.

POTENTIAL: The individual's capacity or aptitude to carry out a certain action or behavior in the future.

PROBLEM-SOLVING: The process involved in arriving at the correct or best answer to a specific problem for which the individual previously did not have a solution.

PROFESSOR'S PERSONALITY: The particular set of personality characteristics of the professor that result in some requirements that his students must meet and, thus, constitute part of the course-demands.

QUESTIONING: The act of not accepting everything as given or of asking questions about something either silently or out loud.

REMEMBERING: Recognition or recall of something for a certain period of time that may be of long or short duration.

ROTE: A type of learning in which the individual attempts to remember something by repeating and repeating it until he has it firmly memorized, so that he can recall it and say it without difficulty.

SELF-DEMANDS: Certain characteristics that represent the individual's uniqueness and which require that he behave in certain ways; these characteristics include Reasons and Goals, Types of Abilities, Types of Learning, Habits, Attitudes, Personality Needs, and Unconscious Factors.

SIGNIFICANT OTHERS: Those people in the individual's life, such as high school teachers, the counselor, the principal, a group leader, or a religious leader, who can make important subjective observations about him.

SOCIAL ABILITY: An ability that is primarily dependent upon the functioning of the individual's personality in interpersonal situations.

SOCIAL HABITS: Behaviors, carried out automatically, that are primarily based upon the non-intellectual aspects of the personality and are used in social situations.

SOCIAL SUCCESS: The individual's attainment of a state in which he is highly accepted and functions well with others socially.

SPEAKING: A way of expressing orally ideas, feelings, attitudes, etc., through language involving, primarily, sound symbols.

STUDENT'S UNIQUENESS: The particular combination of characteristics, such as abilities, interests, achievements, personality needs, attitudes, and values, that makes any one student different from all other students.

SUBSTITUTION: A defense mechanism in which the individual unconsciously gives up his primary goal and instead strives for a secondary goal: one way to do this is to build up one type of activity in place of another that has failed; a second is to shift to a more socially acceptable goal; a third is to accept the goals of others whom he admires.

SUBTLE COURSE-DEMANDS: Requirements that are not easily recognizable, such as the unstated goals and expectations of the professor, his particular personality traits, pressures from other students, required abilities, and required types of learning.

SUPERFICIAL READING: A kind of reading which the individual uses simply to obtain information or, when he is interested only in the plot of a novel, for "escape," as pleasure-reading, etc. The reader is concerned primarily with the "who, what, when, and where" aspects of the material and not with long-time retention of the ideas or application of this reading to other material.

TEACHER EVALUATION: A professor's own way of judging the worth of the student's work; he may do this by averaging the grades for specific tasks such as papers, exams, oral reports, laboratory exercises, etc., or by subjective observation in which grades are assigned according to some standards that he believes students should meet, or by comparing one student's work with the work of other students in the same class.

TRIAL AND ERROR: A type of learning in which behavior changes because the individual tries to do something, makes errors, and finally—practically by accident—finds a solution.

UNCONSCIOUS FACTORS: Those thoughts and feelings that are in the unconscious part of our personality.

UNCONSCIOUS INSIGHT: A type of learning in which the individual learns something without being conscious, at that time, of trying to solve a problem or learn anything; he suddenly discovers a solution to a problem he has been trying to solve for a long period of time; he gets an insight without even thinking about the problem or trying to remember it and finds that he now has no trouble in solving or remembering it.

WITHDRAWAL: A defense mechanism which leads the individual to move away from a frustrating situation; he does this by becoming over-involved in many other activities, by withdrawing into himself psychologically, or by fantasying the reaching of his goals.

WRITING: A way of expressing on paper ideas, feelings, attitudes, etc., through language involving, primarily, verbal symbols.

INDEX

ACTIVITY SHEETS

Activity Sheet 1 • ANALYSIS OF MY HABITS

DIRECTIONS • *Think of the various habits you now have. Decide which of these should help you achieve success in college. List these in the appropriate places. Be sure to be honest with yourself. Covering up your habits will only reduce your chances of changing them!*

Habits Which Should Help College Success

Mental Habits

Social Habits

Physical Habits

Habits Which Should Hinder College Success

Mental Habits

Social Habits

Physical Habits

Activity Sheet 2 • ANALYSIS OF MY ATTITUDES

DIRECTIONS • *Think of your attitudes toward people, work, study, recreation, and your family. Decide which of these will tend to help you achieve college success and label them "positive." Label those that will probably hinder your success "negative." List them in the appropriate spaces.*

_____

Positive

Negative

Activity Sheet 3 • REASONS WHY I AM GOING TO COLLEGE

DIRECTIONS • *List all of the reasons why you are going to college. List not only the ones that you have stated to other people, but also the reasons you have dared to admit only to yourself. Be as specific as possible. Name as many reasons as you can.*

1. _____

2. _____

3. _____

4. _____

5. _____

6. _____

7. _____

8. _____

9. _____

10. _____

11. _____

12. _____

13. _____

14. _____

15. _____

Activity Sheet 4 • **CLASSIFICATION OF MY REASONS FOR GOING TO COLLEGE**

DIRECTIONS • *Study your list of reasons in Activity Sheet 3. After reviewing the definitions of the various types of success presented in Chapter III, list your reasons in the appropriate categories below. If a reason fits more than one category, list it wherever it fits. This procedure will only have value if you are completely honest. Do not try to force your reasons to fit into all categories.*

Category	Reasons*
1. Academic success	_____
2. Artistic success	_____
3. Social success	_____
4. Athletic success	_____
5. Economic success	_____
6. Occupational success	_____

* List your reasons by number, using the numbers by which you have categorized them in Activity Sheet 3.

Activity Sheet 5 • TYPES OF SUCCESS I PREFER

DIRECTIONS • *Study your classification of your reasons for going to college as you have listed them in Activity Sheet 4, and use this information to determine the types of success you prefer. You can do this by identifying the category that has the largest number of reasons listed; this category represents the type of success most important to you. The category with the least number of reasons represents the type of success least important to you. All the remaining categories represent types of success that are moderately important to you. Fill in the following chart with this information.*

_____

Most important type of success to me: _____

Least important type of success to me: _____

Moderately important types of success to me: _____

_____

_____

_____

Activity Sheet 6 • WHY MY COLLEGE EXISTS

DIRECTIONS • *Think of all the possible reasons why your college exists. List below what you at present think are the goals of your college. Do this without sharing your ideas with anyone and without referring to any printed information published by your college. Be as specific as possible.*

1. _____

2. _____

3. _____

4. _____

5. _____

6. _____

7. _____

8. _____

9. _____

10. _____

Activity Sheet 7 • MY COLLEGE'S VIEW OF WHY IT EXISTS

DIRECTIONS • *Obtain copies of your College Bulletin and Freshman Hand-book. From the sections of the Bulletin that discuss the nature of the college, identify what the college's goals are. Do the same for the Handbook. List below as many specific goals or reasons as you can.*

1. _____

2. _____

3. _____

4. _____

5. _____

6. _____

7. _____

8. _____

9. _____

10. _____

Activity Sheet 8 • **CLASSIFYING MY COLLEGE'S REASONS FOR EXISTING**

DIRECTIONS • *Study the list of goals or reasons in Activity Sheet 7. List each of these in the appropriate category below. If a goal or reason fits more than one category, list it wherever it fits. Do not try to force goals or reasons to fit into all categories. If necessary, review the discussion of these categories in Chapter III.*

Category	Reasons*
1. Academic success	_____
2. Artistic success	_____
3. Social success	_____
4. Athletic success	_____
5. Economic success	_____
6. Occupational success	_____

* List your reasons by number, using the numbers by which you have categorized them in Activity Sheet 7.

Activity Sheet 9 • **COMPARING THE TYPES OF SUCCESS WHICH MY COLLEGE AND I PREFER**

DIRECTIONS • *Study the classification you have made in Activity Sheet 8, and identify the category that has the largest number of goals or reasons listed. This category represents the type of success most important to your college. The category with the least number of goals or reasons represents the type of success that is least important to your college. All the remaining categories represent types of success that are moderately important to your college. Fill in the first half of this chart with this information. Following this, complete the chart by transferring the appropriate information from Activity Sheet 5.*

	To My College	*To Me*
Most important type of success:	_____	_____
Least important type of success:	_____	_____
Moderately important types of success:	_____	_____
	_____	_____
	_____	_____
	_____	_____

Activity Sheet 10 • DETERMINING THE GOALS OF ONE OF MY COURSES

DIRECTIONS • *First, look at the description of this course in your College Bulletin and fill in Section I below. Second, study the syllabus and outline of the course, if there is one, and complete Section II below. Third, talk to your instructor and ask him to indicate the course's goals. Although you may be hesitant, most instructors are quite willing to do this. Fill in Section III below. Fourth, talk to several students who have had the same course from the same teacher. (Be sure it is the same teacher, since different professors teaching the same course can have different goals.) Complete Section IV below. Finally, study your information, combine similar goals, and then develop the composite list and fill in Section V.*

Name of Course _____

1. *List of Goals from College Bulletin:*

_____
_____
_____
_____

2. *List of goals from syllabus or outline:*

_____
_____
_____
_____

3. *List of goals from discussion with instructor:*

_____
_____
_____
_____

4. *List of goals from discussion with several students:*

_____
_____
_____
_____

5. *Composite list of course goals from all sources:*

_____
_____
_____
_____
_____
_____

Activity Sheet 11 • DETERMINING THE GOALS OF MY OTHER COURSES

DIRECTIONS • *Following the steps outlined in Activity Sheet 10, fill in the appropriate spaces for each of your current courses.*

_____

Name of Second Course _____

1. *List of goals from College Bulletin:*

_____

_____

_____

_____

2. *List of goals from syllabus or outline:*

_____

_____

_____

_____

3. *List of goals from discussion with instructor:*

_____

_____

_____

_____

4. *List of goals from discussion with several students:*

_____

_____

_____

_____

5. *Composite list of course goals from all sources:*

_____

_____

_____

_____

_____

_____

Activity Sheet 11—Continued

_____

Name of Third Course _____

1. *List of goals from College Bulletin:*

_____
_____
_____
_____

2. *List of goals from syllabus or outline:*

_____
_____
_____
_____

3. *List of goals from discussion with instructor:*

_____
_____
_____
_____

4. *List of goals from discussion with several students:*

_____
_____
_____
_____

5. *Composite list of course goals from all sources:*

_____
_____
_____
_____
_____
_____
_____

Activity Sheet 11—Continued

Name of Fourth Course _____

1. *List of goals from College Bulletin:*

_____

_____

_____

_____

2. *List of goals from syllabus or outline:*

_____

_____

_____

_____

3. *List of goals from discussion with instructor:*

_____

_____

_____

_____

4. *List of goals from discussion with several students:*

_____

_____

_____

_____

5. *Composite list of course goals from all sources:*

_____

_____

_____

_____

_____

_____

Activity Sheet 11—Continued

Name of Fifth Course _____

1. *List of goals from College Bulletin:*

_____
_____
_____
_____

2. *List of goals from syllabus or outline:*

_____
_____
_____
_____

3. *List of goals from discussion with instructor:*

_____
_____
_____
_____

4. *List of goals from discussion with several students:*

_____
_____
_____
_____

5. *Composite list of course goals from all sources:*

_____
_____
_____
_____
_____
_____

Activity Sheet 12 • **COMPARISON OF MY REASONS FOR GOING TO COLLEGE AND MY COURSES' GOALS**

DIRECTIONS • *Analyze the composite lists of your courses' goals listed in Activity Sheets 10 and 11. Identify similar ones and list these in the left-hand column below. Identify different ones that seem to be particularly important for one of your courses. List these in the left-hand column also. From Activity Sheet 3, list in the right-hand column your reasons for going to college. Compare the two columns to determine their degree of similarity. Do this by counting the number of similar statements and determining the percentage of similarity. State the degree of agreement in the appropriate space according to this key:*

Percentage of Similarity	Degree of Agreement
76%–100%	Very High
51%– 75%	High
26%– 50%	Moderate
0%– 25%	Low

Composite Listing of My Current Courses' Goals	My Reasons for Going to College
1.	1.
2.	2.
3.	3.
4.	4.
5.	5.
6.	6.
7.	7.
8.	8.
9.	9.
10.	10.
11.	11.
12.	12.
13.	13.
14.	14.
15.	15.

Degree of agreement between the two lists: _____

Activity Sheet 13 • DETERMINING MY ABILITIES FROM MY HIGH SCHOOL RECORD

DIRECTIONS • *Think about what you have done while in high school. Analyze the activities you carried out well and those you did not do well. Categorize them in terms of mental, physical, or social abilities. List them in the appropriate spaces below. If you have difficulty doing this, review David's analysis presented in Chapter IV.*

Highest Abilities	*Lowest Abilities*
Mental	*Mental*
1. _____	1. _____
2. _____	2. _____
3. _____	3. _____
4. _____	4. _____
5. _____	5. _____
Physical	*Physical*
1. _____	1. _____
2. _____	2. _____
3. _____	3. _____
4. _____	4. _____
5. _____	5. _____
Social	*Social*
1. _____	1. _____
2. _____	2. _____
3. _____	3. _____
4. _____	4. _____
5. _____	5. _____

Activity Sheet 14 • DETERMINING MY ABILITIES FROM MY NON-SCHOOL ACTIVITIES

DIRECTIONS • *Think about the various non-school activities you were involved in during the last three years. These might include clubs and informal groups in which you participated. Consider also any religious group, athletic team, social group, and home activities in which you were involved. Decide which of these you typically carried out well and those you did not do well. Categorize them in terms of mental, physical, or social abilities, and list them below.*

Highest Abilities	*Lowest Abilities*

Mental

1. _____
2. _____
3. _____
4. _____
5. _____

Physical

1. _____
2. _____
3. _____
4. _____
5. _____

Social

1. _____
2. _____
3. _____
4. _____
5. _____

Mental

1. _____
2. _____
3. _____
4. _____
5. _____

Physical

1. _____
2. _____
3. _____
4. _____
5. _____

Social

1. _____
2. _____
3. _____
4. _____
5. _____

Activity Sheet 15 • DETERMINING MY ABILITIES FROM TEST RESULTS

DIRECTIONS • *Confer with your high school or college counselor concerning your performance on any standardized ability and achievement tests you have taken. Be sure to explain why you want this information. After he has explained the meaning of these results, fill in the spaces below.*

Highest Mental Abilities	Lowest Mental Abilities

Ability Tests

1. _____

2. _____

3. _____

4. _____

5. _____

Ability Tests

1. _____

2. _____

3. _____

4. _____

5. _____

Achievement Tests

1. _____

2. _____

3. _____

4. _____

5. _____

Achievement Tests

1. _____

2. _____

3. _____

4. _____

5. _____

Activity Sheet 16 • **DETERMINING MY ABILITIES FROM OTHERS' OBSERVATIONS**

DIRECTIONS • *Make an analysis of the subjective observations of your teachers, counselor, principal, religious leader, and so on. You can do this by interviewing these people and telling them you are trying to obtain a better understanding of your highest and lowest abilities. Explain to them that you would like their honest evaluations so that you can obtain other people's views of yourself. After doing this, categorize your information and fill in the spaces below.*

Highest Abilities	Lowest Abilities
Mental	*Mental*
1. _____	1. _____
2. _____	2. _____
3. _____	3. _____
4. _____	4. _____
5. _____	5. _____
Physical	*Physical*
1. _____	1. _____
2. _____	2. _____
3. _____	3. _____
4. _____	4. _____
5. _____	5. _____
Social	*Social*
1. _____	1. _____
2. _____	2. _____
3. _____	3. _____
4. _____	4. _____
5. _____	5. _____

Activity Sheet 17 • SUMMARY LISTING OF MY HIGHEST AND LOWEST ABILITIES

DIRECTIONS • *Based upon the information you obtained in Activity Sheets 13–16, identify your most common highest and lowest abilities. List these in the appropriate spaces below.*

Highest Abilities

Mental

1. _____
2. _____
3. _____
4. _____
5. _____
6. _____
7. _____
8. _____
9. _____
10. _____

Physical

1. _____
2. _____
3. _____
4. _____
5. _____
6. _____
7. _____
8. _____
9. _____
10. _____

Social

1. _____
2. _____
3. _____
4. _____
5. _____
6. _____
7. _____
8. _____
9. _____
10. _____

Activity Sheet 17—Continued

Lowest Abilities

Mental

1. _____
2. _____
3. _____
4. _____
5. _____
6. _____
7. _____
8. _____
9. _____
10. _____

Physical

1. _____
2. _____
3. _____
4. _____
5. _____
6. _____
7. _____
8. _____
9. _____
10. _____

Social

1. _____
2. _____
3. _____
4. _____
5. _____
6. _____
7. _____
8. _____
9. _____
10. _____

Activity Sheet 18 • **PRELIMINARY LIST OF ABILITIES REQUIRED AT MY COLLEGE**

DIRECTIONS • *Develop this preliminary list from the information included in Activity Sheet 7. Analyze each of your college's goals which is listed there and determine the ability or abilities needed to achieve it. If you need help, review the discussion presented in Chapter IV. Categorize each ability and list it in the appropriate spaces below.*

Mental

1. _____

2. _____

3. _____

4. _____

5. _____

Physical

1. _____

2. _____

3. _____

4. _____

5. _____

Social

1. _____

2. _____

3. _____

4. _____

5. _____

Activity Sheet 19 • SECOND LISTING OF ABILITIES REQUIRED AT MY COLLEGE

DIRECTIONS • *This listing is to be developed from your previous analysis of your current courses' goals. Using the informaton from Activity Sheet 12, figure out the mental, social, and physical abilities required to achieve the stated goals of your courses. If necessary, review the discussion in Chapter IV of the process needed to do this. Fill in the appropriate spaces below with this information.*

Mental

1. _____
2. _____
3. _____
4. _____
5. _____
6. _____
7. _____
8. _____
9. _____
10. _____

Physical

1. _____
2. _____
3. _____
4. _____
5. _____

Social

1. _____
2. _____
3. _____
4. _____
5. _____

Activity Sheet 20 • FINAL LISTING OF ABILITIES REQUIRED AT MY COLLEGE

DIRECTIONS • *This final listing is to be derived from your first two lists of required abilities in Activity Sheets 18 and 19. Identify similar statements and list them below in the appropriate spaces. Also list all other statements from both Activity Sheets.*

Mental

1. _____
2. _____
3. _____
4. _____
5. _____
6. _____
7. _____
8. _____
9. _____
10. _____

Physical

1. _____
2. _____
3. _____
4. _____
5. _____
6. _____
7. _____
8. _____
9. _____
10. _____

Social

1. _____
2. _____
3. _____
4. _____
5. _____
6. _____
7. _____
8. _____
9. _____
10. _____

Activity Sheet 21 • COMPARISON OF MY HIGHEST ABILITIES AND THE ABILITIES REQUIRED AT MY COLLEGE

DIRECTIONS • *Using your information from Activity Sheet 17, analyze the nature of your highest abilities. Compare these to the final listing of abilities required at your college (Activity Sheet 20). Pick out the similarities and differences between your highest abilities and those required by your college. Fill in the spaces below and on the following page with this information.*

My Highest Abilities Which Are Similar to Required Abilities

Mental

1. _____

2. _____

3. _____

4. _____

5. _____

Physical

1. _____

2. _____

3. _____

4. _____

5. _____

Social

1. _____

2. _____

3. _____

4. _____

5. _____

Activity Sheet 21—Continued

My Highest Abilities Which Are Different from Required Abilities

Mental

1. _____

2. _____

3. _____

4. _____

5. _____

Physical

1. _____

2. _____

3. _____

4. _____

5. _____

Social

1. _____

2. _____

3. _____

4. _____

5. _____

Activity Sheet 22 • **PRELIMINARY LISTING OF TYPES OF LEARNING REQUIRED AT MY COLLEGE**

DIRECTIONS • *Analyze your list of your current courses' goals.* Based upon the discussion in Chapter IV, check the types of learning required for each stated goal.*

Composite Listing of Current Courses' Goals*	Types of Learning				
	Trial and Error	Rote	Association	Conscious Problem-Solving	Unconscious Insight
1.					
2.					
3.					
4.					
5.					
6.					
7.					
8.					
9.					
10.					

* Obtain from Activity Sheet 12.

Activity Sheet 23 • SECOND LISTING OF TYPES OF LEARNING REQUIRED AT MY COLLEGE

DIRECTIONS • *Analyze your list of the abilities required at your college.* Referring to the discussion in Chapter IV, check where appropriate the types of learning required for each stated ability.*

Required Abilities at My College*	Types of Learning				
	Trial and Error	Rote	Association	Conscious Problem-Solving	Unconscious Insight

Mental

1. ___
2. ___
3. ___
4. ___
5. ___
6. ___
7. ___
8. ___
9. ___
10. ___

Physical

1. ___
2. ___
3. ___
4. ___
5. ___
6. ___
7. ___
8. ___
9. ___
10. ___

Social

1. ___
2. ___
3. ___
4. ___
5. ___
6. ___
7. ___
8. ___
9. ___
10. ___

* Obtain from Activity Sheet 20.

**Activity Sheet 24 • FINAL LISTING OF TYPES OF LEARNING REQUIRED
AT MY COLLEGE**

DIRECTIONS • *Analyze Activity Sheets 22 and 23. Identify the types of
learning frequently checked. List these in the appropriate spaces below. Do the
same for the types of learning checked least often. Finally, list those which remain
as moderately required.*

_____

Types of learning frequently required:

_____

_____

_____

Types of learning least required:

_____

_____

_____

Types of learning moderately required:

_____

_____

_____

_____

Activity Sheet 25 • TYPES OF LEARNING I PREFER

DIRECTIONS • *Using the discussion in Chapter IV as a guide, determine the types of learning you prefer. First analyze the way you study and fill in the spaces below with your conclusions. Do the same for your reactions to your courses and your analysis of your non-school situations. From this information, identify the preferred types of learning most frequently stated and list them.*

_____

From analysis of study procedures:

_____

_____

From analysis of courses:

_____

_____

From analysis of non-school situations:

_____

_____

Composite list of preferences:

_____

_____

_____

_____

Activity Sheet 26 • TYPES OF LEARNING I USE BEST

DIRECTIONS • *Using the discussion in Chapter IV as a guide, determine the types of learning you handle best. First, analyze your achievement in your various high school or college courses. Identify the types of learning which you have used best and list them below. Second, analyze your non-school activities. After identifying the types of learning which have produced the best results, list them below. Finally, determine the types most frequently listed and fill in the appropriate spaces.*

_____

From analysis of courses:

_____

_____

From analysis of non-school situations:

_____

_____

Composite list from above:

_____

_____

_____

Activity Sheet 27 • COMPARISON OF PREFERRED AND BEST TYPES OF LEARNING

DIRECTIONS • *Using the composite lists from Activity Sheets 25 and 26, determine the types of learning you prefer and use best. List them in the appropriate spaces below. Next, identify the types of learning you prefer but do not use best. List these also. Finally, identify the types of learning you use best but do not prefer. List them last.*

_____

Types of learning I prefer AND do best:

_____

_____

_____

Types of learning I prefer but do NOT do best:

_____

_____

_____

Types of learning I do best but do NOT prefer:

_____

_____

_____

_____

Activity Sheet 28 • COMPARISON OF TYPES OF LEARNING: MY COLLEGE AND ME

DIRECTIONS • *Using Activity Sheet 24, identify the types of learning frequently and moderately required at your college. List these in the left-hand column below. From Activity Sheet 27, determine the types of learning you prefer and use best. List these in the right-hand column below. Note the similarities and differences.*

Types of Learning Frequently and Moderately Required at My College	*Types of Learning I Prefer and Use Best*
1. _____	1. _____
2. _____	2. _____
3. _____	3. _____
4. _____	4. _____

Activity Sheet 29 • **DETERMINING THE COURSE-DEMANDS OF ONE OF MY COURSES**

DIRECTIONS • *In line with the discussion in Chapter V, collect all the information you will need for this analysis. This will include information from your College Bulletin, the printed course descriptions available, and statements by your professor regarding the course's requirements. In addition note your observations of your professor and your fellow students. Finally, keep handy your previously determined lists of your course's goals, abilities, and required types of learning as they are incorporated in Activity Sheets 10, 11, 19, and 22.*

Using this information, begin identifying Activities. As you discover appropriate data, list them in the accompanying chart. Be sure to analyze each source of information and list your findings in the appropriate spaces. After completing this process for Activities, move on to Regulations. Do the same for the other categories of course-demands. If you run into difficulties, review the discussion of this procedure as it was presented in Chapter V.

Course-Demand	College Bulletin (1)	Printed Course Description (2)	Oral Course Description (3)
Activities (A)			
Regulations (B)			

Activity Sheet 29—Continued

Observations of Professor (4)	Observations of Students (5)	Previously Listed Goals (6)	Previously Listed Abilities and Learnings (7)

Activity Sheet 29—Continued

Course-Demand	College Bulletin (1)	Printed Course Description (2)	Oral Course Description (3)
Goals (C)			
Types of Abilities (D)			
Types of Learning (E)			

Activity Sheet 29—Continued

Observations of Professor (4)	Observations of Students (5)	Previously Listed Goals (6)	Previously Listed Abilities and Learnings (7)

Activity Sheet 29—Continued

Course-Demand	College Bulletin (1)	Printed Course Description (2)	Oral Course Description (3)
Teacher Evaluation (F)			
Professor's Personality (G)			
Student Pressure (H)			

Activity Sheet 29—Continued

Observations of Professor (4)	Observations of Students (5)	Previously Listed Goals (6)	Previously Listed Abilities and Learnings (7)

Activity Sheet 30 • **COMPOSITE STATEMENT OF THE COURSE-DEMANDS FOR ONE OF MY COURSES**

DIRECTIONS • *Analyze the data in Activity Sheet 29. Notice the overlapping and repetition in certain categories resulting from the various sources of information used. For each course-demand, eliminate the duplications and combine the remaining information. Where duplications exist, show this by using the following code system: At the end of each statement add*
    1—if considerable duplication exists in sources
    2—if some duplication exists in sources
    3—if no duplication exists in sources.
If you have difficulties, review the discussion of this procedure as it is presented in Chapter V.

Course-Demand	Statement
Activities (A)	
Regulations (B)	
Goals (C)	

Activity Sheet 30—Continued

Course-Demand	Statement
Types of Abilities (D)	
Types of Learning (E)	
Teacher Evaluation (F)	
Professor's Personality (G)	
Student Pressure (H)	

Activity Sheet 31 • **DETERMINING MY SELF-DEMANDS**

DIRECTIONS • *In line with the discussion in Chapter VI, collect all the information you will need for this analysis. Begin by having available Activity Sheets 1–5, 13–20, 25, and 26. They include your preliminary analyses of your reasons for going to college, your habits, attitudes, highest and lowest abilities, and the types of learning you prefer and use best.*

Your next step is to gather all the additional information you will need to fill out the accompanying chart. Do this by following the procedures discussed in Chapter VI, concerning the use of Self, High School Record, Non-School Activities, Test Results, Significant Others, College Personnel, and College Record.

After you have these data, proceed by identifying your Reasons and Goals. As you discover appropriate data, list them in the proper space. Be sure to analyze each source of information and list all the suitable statements. After completing this process for Reasons and Goals, proceed to Types of Abilities. Do the same for the other categories of self-demands. If you have any difficulties, review the discussion of this procedure presented in Chapter VI.

Self-Demand	Source of Information		
	Self (1)	High School Record (2)	Non-School Activities (3)
Reasons and Goals (A)			
Types of Abilities (B) — Highest	Mental		
	Physical		
	Social		

Activity Sheet 31—Continued

	Source of Information		
Test Results (4)	Significant Others (5)	College Personnel (6)	College Record (7)

Mental

Physical

Social

Activity Sheet 31—Continued

Self-Demand	Source of Information		
	Self (1)	High School Record (2)	Non-School Activities (3)
Types of Abilities (B) — Lowest	Mental		
	Physical		
	Social		
Types of Learning (C)	Prefer		
	Do Best		
Habits (D) — To Help	Mental		
	Social		
	Physical		

Activity Sheet 31—Continued

	Source of Information			
	Test Results (4)	Significant Others (5)	College Personnel (6)	College Record (7)
Mental				
Physical				
Social				
Prefer				
Do Best				
Mental				
Social				
Physical				

Activity Sheet 31—Continued

Self-Demand		Source of Information		
		Self (1)	High School Record (2)	Non-School Activities (3)
Habits (D) — To Hinder	*Mental*			
	Social			
	Physical			
Attitudes (E)	*Positive*			
	Negative			
Personality Needs (F)	*Biological*			
	Psychological			

Activity Sheet 31—Continued

	Source of Information			
	Test Results (4)	Significant Others (5)	College Personnel (6)	College Record (7)
Mental				
Social				
Physical				
Positive				
Negative				
Biological				
Psychological				

Activity Sheet 31—Continued

Self-Demand	Source of Information		
	Self (1)	High School Record (2)	Non-School Activities (3)
Unconscious Factors (G)			

Activity Sheet 31—Continued

Source of Information			
Test Results (4)	Significant Others (5)	College Personnel (6)	College Record (7)

Activity Sheet 32 • COMPOSITE STATEMENT OF MY SELF-DEMANDS

DIRECTIONS • *Analyze the data in Activity Sheet 31. Notice the overlapping and repetition in certain categories resulting from the various sources of information used. For each self-demand, eliminate the duplications and combine the remaining information. List these statements in the accompanying chart. Where duplications exist, show this by using the following code system. At the end of each statement add:*

    1—if considerable duplication exists in sources
    2—if some duplication exists in sources
    3—if no duplication exists in sources.

    If you have difficulties, review the discussion of this procedure presented in Chapter VI.

Self-Demand	Statement
Reasons and Goals (A)	
Types of Abilities (B) — Highest	Mental
	Physical
	Social
Types of Abilities (B) — Lowest	Mental
	Physical
	Social
Types of Learning (C)	Prefer
	Do Best

Activity Sheet 32—Continued

Self-Demand		Statement
Habits (D) — Which Help	Mental	
	Social	
	Physical	
Habits (D) — Which Hinder	Mental	
	Social	
	Physical	
Attitudes (E)	Positive	
	Negative	
Personality Needs (F)	Biological	
	Psychological	
Unconscious Factors (G)		

Activity Sheet 33 • COMPARING MY SELF-DEMANDS WITH MY COURSE-DEMANDS

DIRECTIONS • *Have available Activity Sheets 30 and 32. Review the information on course-demands. Look carefully at the list of Activities. With these in mind, review the self-demands information. Read each statement carefully to see if it seems to fit the statements of the course-demands in the Activity category. When a statement fits, list it in Column (1) of the accompanying chart. Also list the source of information (self-demand) in Column (2). Now do the same thing for the statements of self-demands that do not fit the Activities statements. List the data in Column (3) and the source of information for each in Column (4).*

Repeat the above steps for each of the remaining course-demands. Start with Regulations and proceed until you finish with Student Pressure. If you encounter any difficulties, review the discussion of David's self-demands and course-demands which is presented in Chapter VII.

Name of Course: _____

Course-Demand	Self-Demands Which Fit Course-Demands	
	Specific Data (1)	Source of Information (2)
Activities (A)		
Regulations (B)		

Activity Sheet 33—Continued

Course-Demand	Self-Demands Which Do Not Fit Course-Demands	
	Specific Data (3)	*Source of Information* (4)
Activities (A)		
Regulations (B)		

Activity Sheet 33—Continued

Course-Demand	Self-Demands Which Fit Course-Demands	
	Specific Data (1)	Source of Information (2)
Goals (C)		
Types of Abilities (D)		
Types of Learning (E)		

Activity Sheet 33—Continued

Course-Demand	Self-Demands Which Do Not Fit Course-Demands	
	Specific Data (3)	Source of Information (4)
Goals (C)		
Types of Abilities (D)		
Types of Learning (E)		

Activity Sheet 33—Continued

Course-Demand	Self-Demands Which Fit Course-Demands	
	Specific Data (1)	Source of Information (2)
Teacher Evaluation (F)		
Professor's Personality (G)		
Student Pressure (H)		

Activity Sheet 33—Continued

Course-Demand	Self-Demands Which Do Not Fit Course-Demands	
	Specific Data (3)	Source of Information (4)
Teacher Evaluation (F)		
Professor's Personality (G)		
Student Pressure (H)		

Activity Sheet 34 • MY SELF-DEMANDS THAT MOST FREQUENTLY FIT MY COURSE-DEMANDS

DIRECTIONS • *Using Activity Sheet 33, identify your self-demands that most frequently fit your course-demands. Do this by counting the number of times each statement of a self-demand is listed in Column (1) for all of the categories. Identify and list the statements of self-demands that are listed for at least four different course-demands. After this, list the identified statements in the appropriate spaces below. Review the discussion in Chapter VII if you have any difficulties.*

Self-Demand	Specific Data
Reasons and Goals (A)	
Types of Abilities (B)	
Types of Learning (C)	
Habits (D)	
Attitudes (E)	
Personality Needs (F)	
Unconscious Factors (G)	

Activity Sheet 35 • SUMMARY COMPARISON OF MY SELF-DEMANDS WITH MY COURSE-DEMANDS

DIRECTIONS • *Using Activity Sheet 33, determine the degree to which your self-demands meet your course-demands. Do this by checking the appropriate spaces below according to the following code:*

GREAT: *if all or almost all of the data on self-demands were placed in Column (1) as compared to Column (3)*

MODERATE: *if most of the data on self-demands were placed in Column (1) as compared to Column (3)*

SLIGHT: *if about equal amounts of the data on self-demands were placed in Columns (1) and (3)*

NEGATIVE: *if all or almost all of the data on self-demands were placed in Column (3) as compared to Column (1).*

If you encounter problems in making this analysis, review the discussion in Chapter VII.

Course-Demand	Extent to Which My Self-Demands Fit My Course-Demands			
	Great (1)	Moderate (2)	Slight (3)	Negative (4)
Activities (A)				
Regulations (B)				
Goals (C)				
Types of Abilities (D)				
Types of Learning (E)				
Teacher Evaluation (F)				
Professor's Personality (G)				
Student Pressure (H)				

Activity Sheet 36 • MY SELF-DEMANDS THAT DO NOT FIT MY COURSE-DEMANDS

DIRECTIONS • *Using Activity Sheet 33, identify your self-demands that do not fit your course-demands. List all of the statements from Column (3) in the appropriate spaces below. Identify those listed for more than one course-demand by adding the number one (1) after each appropriate statement. Identify the most frequently listed statement by adding the number two (2) after that statement. Consult the discussion in Chapter VII if you have difficulties.*

Self-Demand	Specific Data
Reasons and Goals (A)	
Types of Abilities (B)	
Types of Learning (C)	
Habits (D)	
Attitudes (E)	
Personality Needs (F)	
Unconscious Factors (G)	

Activity Sheet 37 • PLAN OF ACTION FOR MODIFYING MY SELF-DEMANDS

DIRECTIONS • *Before developing your plan of action to modify your self-demands, you should make sure your completed analyses are still accurate. After studying Chapters VIII–XIII, review Activity Sheets 29–36. Make any necessary corrections.*

Assuming that these Activity Sheets are now complete, keep them before you as you follow these steps. First, list in Column (1b) of the accompanying chart any problems you notice for each of your self-demands that do not fit your course-demands. You can accomplish this by studying Activity Sheet 36 and deciding on the nature of the problems. If you have difficulty doing this, review the steps David followed in our discussion in Chapter XIII.

Second, think of several specific procedures you can carry out to remedy each problem. These procedures should be based upon the material presented in Chapters VIII through XIII. For each problem review the possible methods discussed there. Be sure the procedures you identify are suitable to you! You should consider all of your self-demands as you plan to modify one of them. The procedures should also be consistent with each other. List these procedures in Column (2) opposite each stated problem.

As you develop this plan of action, keep in mind that you will probably have to revise it later. Therefore, do not be too concerned about selecting the "correct" procedures. You should anticipate making errors. This is not crucial, since you will appraise your progress later. The most important thing is that you take steps to modify your self-demands. You can correct your errors as you go along.

Third, carry out your plan of action for at least two weeks. If possible, follow it through for a month. Be sure to keep your plan in mind as this time period proceeds.

Fourth, after several weeks have passed appraise the results of your efforts. Write in your observations in Column (3). Be sure to note failures as well as successes. Indicate what you have actually done in comparison to what you had planned to do.

Fifth, following this appraisal revise your plan of action. In view of the failures, think of additional means of modifying your self-demands. List these in the appropriate spaces. If you run out of ideas, consult your advisor or counselor.

Finally, repeat steps three and four as often as necessary. Use additional sheets of paper, if necessary, to record your efforts.

Self-Demand Needing Modification		Plan to Modify This Self-Demand (2)	Results of Attempts to Modify This Self-Demand (3)
Self-Demand (1a)	Problem (1b)		
Reasons and Goals (A)			

Activity Sheet 37—Continued

Self-Demand Needing Modification		Plan to Modify This Self-Demand (2)	Results of Attempts to Modify This Self-Demand (3)
Self-Demand (1a)	Problem (1b)		
Types of Abilities (B)			
Types of Learning (C)			
Habits (D)			

Activity Sheet 37—Continued

Self-Demand Needing Modification		Plan to Modify This Self-Demand (2)	Results of Attempts to Modify This Self-Demand (3)
Self-Demand (1a)	Problem (1b)		
Attitudes (E)			
Personality Needs (F)			
Unconscious Factors (G)			